EFFECTIVE
SALES
INCENTIVE
COMPENSATION

JOHN W. BARRY
PORTER HENRY

EFFECTIVE SALES INCENTIVE COMPENSATION

McGRAW-HILL BOOK COMPANY

New York St. Louis San Francisco Auckland Bogotá
Hamburg Johannesburg London Madrid Mexico
Montreal New Delhi Panama Paris São Paulo
Singapore Sydney Tokyo Toronto

Library of Congress Cataloging in Publication Data

Barry, John W   1905-
  Effective sales incentive compensation.

  Includes index.
  1. Sales personnel—Salaries, commissions, etc.
2. Incentives in industry.   I. Henry, Porter, joint
author.   II. Title.
HF5439.7.B37   658.3'225   80-18603
ISBN 0-07-003860-0

1 2 3 4 5 6 7 8 9 0   BP   BP   8 9 8 7 6 5 4 3 2 1

The editors for this book were William Newton and Ann
Gray, the designer was Elliot Epstein, and the production
supervisor was Paul Malchow. It was set in Electra and
Souvenir Light by the Elizabeth Typesetting Company.

It was printed and bound by The Book Press.

CONTENTS

v

PREFACE

The chaotic economic conditions of the past few years have necessitated revisions in most sales incentive compensation plans. A succession of booms and "stagflations" has made it difficult to motivate the sales force and at the same time maintain a satisfactory profit margin.

Inflation and higher tax brackets have created a demand for larger incentive payments, while the slowdown in industries like automobiles and housing has underlined the importance of the security provided by the fixed portion of sales force income.

This book is written as a guide for those companies which take a do-it-yourself approach toward the revision or overhaul of their sales compensation plans.

A plan that works well for one company may be a disaster for another company, even a similar one. Hence this book contains no model plans, but instead develops the principles a sales executive can follow in imaginatively creating a plan to fit the company's needs at this point in time.

The coverage of this book is broad. It discusses the rationale of sales incentive plans; the importance of clarifying their objectives; methods of evaluating an existing plan; factors to be considered in revising the plan or designing a new one; ways of meshing incentives with salaries; and ways of testing, introducing, and capitalizing on the plan. The book covers compensation plans for field sales executives, as well as for wholesalers and retailers.

Because the book stresses the role of sales compensation as a marketing tool, it should be of interest to marketing executives as well as to sales executives. And since it emphasizes the effects of compensation plans upon corporate profits, it will also be of value to financial executives.

Other books dealing with sales incentive compensation tend to stress the aspects of salary administration, with less attention to the variety of available incentive methods and their use as a sales tool.

Much of the literature on the subject has been in the form of magazine articles or brief pamphlets, which unfortunately tempt the busy executive to copy a plan that was successful elsewhere but may not be appropriate to his or her specific requirements.

This book covers both the general concepts and the practical details. Sales incentive compensation needs above all to be considered pragmatically. Theories are much less important than considerations as to what works and what doesn't work.

In preparing this book the authors have been fortunate in being able to draw upon the resources of research organizations such as the American Management Association and the Conference Board, as well as upon the accumulated wisdom of sales executives and consultants, especially B. K. Moffitt and Dean H. Rosenthal. We are grateful to Robert Albert, editor of *Sales and Marketing Management* magazine, for conducting the survey of current incentive practices incorporated into this book.

John W. Barry
Porter Henry

ONE

BACKGROUND

1

WHY BOTHER?

A properly designed sales incentive compensation plan can make a marked contribution to a company's profitability. The phrase "incentive compensation" is here used to refer to any plan which puts additional dollars in the pockets of the sales force as a reward for better sales results. If the plan is carefully tailored to fit the nature of the sales tasks and the objectives of the company, it not only encourages salespersons to work harder but, equally important, it directs their efforts toward the most profitable products and markets.

Motivating the sales rep is different from motivating a bookkeeper or a drill-press operator. The sales job is different. While other employees of the company work in groups having continuous contact with a supervisor, the sales rep leads an essentially lonely and more loosely supervised existence.

The sales rep is constantly subjected to "demotivation" as the best-laid plans and carefully prepared sales presentations fail for reasons beyond the rep's control. The rep's call objectives may be achieved in one call out of four; this means that three times out of four, hopes are frustrated and the ego is bruised. Moreover, hours are irregular and family life is interrupted if much travel is required.

Some compensation consultants who try to squeeze the sales force into a companywide salary administration program increase the base pay of the sales force by 5 percent or so to compensate for the isolated nature of the work.

The authors prefer a compensation plan developed specifically for the sales force.

Skeptics sometimes say that money isn't everything, and cite surveys made among production workers revealing that money usually ranks sixth or seventh from the top on lists of factors which affect production and morale. But to most sales reps, money is desirable not only in its own right, but also as a means of filling psychological needs.

If the sales rep craves recognition, the larger paycheck is a token of the company's recognition of accomplishments. If the rep is achievement-oriented, money is a token of achievement. If the rep is strongly family-oriented, the larger income assures a better education and a better start in life for the children. If the rep is security-minded, investments can make retirement years more comfortable.

Most sales reps will work both harder and smarter if the potential rewards are substantial. The nature of the sales compensation plan thus has a direct and major effect upon profitability.

Yet many companies, and in some cases entire industries, stumble along with plans that either fail to motivate the sales force or motivate it to do the wrong things. A poorly conceived plan can actually work against the objectives it was intended to fulfill. Consider two examples:

> A company manufacturing housewares couldn't understand why every other year was disappointing. Although sales volume was tending upward, there was a definite roller coaster pattern, with good years and bad years alternating.
>
> The sales force was paid a salary, with a year-end bonus based on sales over quota. For every 1 percent by which sales exceeded quota, the sales representative got a bonus equal to 1 percent of salary, up to a maximum of 50 percent of salary. If the base salary was $20,000, a sales rep could earn an additional $10,000 by exceeding quota by 50 percent.
>
> Although the cause of the up-and-down pattern wasn't apparent to anyone sitting in headquarters, a little fieldwork soon revealed it. This was a classic example of an incentive compensation plan with a built-in incentive for the sales force to load distributors up to their ears at year end. Distributors spent most of the next year working off excess inventory, so new purchases were down.
>
> True, the sales rep, by maximizing this year's income, might be taking something off next year's—but if the rep was over quota this year, it made sense to maximize the bonus; next year it might be harder to achieve quota.
>
> The solution was to put all quotas and bonuses on a quarterly basis. The sales rep received a small bonus for each quarter over quota, but a much larger consistency bonus if all four quarters were over quota. The sales rep maximized income by selling consistently throughout the year instead of loading dealers during the last quarter.
>
> Another example of a typical built-in booby trap in a compensation plan concerns a company making electrical equipment. Total sales volume was just about keeping pace

with growth in gross national product, but profits were on a plateau and a promising new specialty product that had been launched two years earlier was withering on the vine.

The marketing director wondered whether the sales force was somehow at fault. The problem shouldn't be one of inadequate motivation. The reps were paid good salaries and could earn an additional 25 percent in incentive payments. These incentives were based on total dollar volume over quotas, and quotas were set fairly.

But the company decided to take a new look at its compensation plan. Two of its best sales reps had left to join competitors. The company learned that while their total income had been keeping pace with inflation, the larger number of dollars put them in a higher tax bracket, and the after-tax portion of the 25 percent bonus didn't look as good as the more modest compensation package offered by the competitor.

More importantly, the entire sales force could earn more money by concentrating on the less profitable run-of-the-mill products than by pushing the new, more profitable product.

As a hypothetical example, let's say that the new A product line contributed 40 percent of each sales dollar to overhead and profit, while the older commodity-type B product contributed only 20 percent. Assume that a sales rep has a quota of $750,000 in sales volume per year, with a bonus of 1 percent on sales over quota. His present sales volume (Table 1-1) is $250,000 of product A and $500,000 of product B.

TABLE 1-1   Present Sales

Product	Sales volume	% contri-bution	Contri-bution	Bonus
A	$250,000	40	$100,000	
B	500,000	20	100,000	
Total	$750,000		$200,000	0

TABLE 1-2   Emphasis on Product B

Product	Sales volume	% contri-bution	Contri-bution	Bonus
A	$ 250,000	40	$100,000	
B	800,000	20	160,000	
Total	$1,050,000		$260,000	$3,000

TABLE 1-3   Emphasis on Product A

Product	Sales volume	% contri-bution	Contri-bution	Bonus
A	$450,000	40	$180,000	
B	500,000	20	100,000	
Total	$950,000		$280,000	$2,000

Motivated by the incentive program, the rep determines to invest additional time and effort. Since it takes about 50 percent more time to sell the A line than the B line, the rep can sell either $300,000 additional B products or $200,000 additional A products.

If the B product is pushed (Table 1-2), the rep will sell an additional $300,000 of it for a total of $800,000, generate a $260,000 contribution, and earn a bonus of $3,000 (1 percent of the $300,000 over the $750,000 quota).

If the more proifitable A product is pushed (Table 1-3), the rep will sell an additional $200,000 of it for a total of $450,000, generate $280,000 in contribution, but receive only a $2,000 bonus. As a reward for increasing the company's profit by $20,000, the rep is penalized $1,000.

To make matters worse, sales and quotas are pooled on a district basis. Therefore any sales reps who exert extra effort to promote the more profitable line not only reduce their own income, but also diminish that of fellow sales reps.

The solution in this case, of course, is to inaugurate a compensation plan which pays a higher percentage bonus on the more profitable product, pays enough of a bonus to provide real after-tax motivation, and rewards each sales rep on the basis of individual productivity.

The incentive plan usually needs to be tailored to the individual company. Two firms selling similar products to identical customers may be quite different in the degree of supervision provided, the kind of nonselling functions required, and the amount of paperwork generated. A good plan for company X may be a bust for competing company Y.

In other cases, plans which were logical and effective five years ago may be completely obsolete now because of the effects of inflation, income taxes, or changes in the industry marketing patterns. A large proportion of existing sales compensation plans need to be reevaluated and revised or, in some cases, scrapped in favor of new plans.

Inexpert tinkering with a compensation plan frequently does more harm than good. While it's true that a sound plan may require frequent minor revisions, it creates sheer frustration for a company to announce, with fanfare and drum beating, a whole new compensation method every two or three years.

How can the compensation plan be evaluated, revised if necessary, or discarded in favor of a new one?

One answer is to turn to a consultant who specializes in sales compensation programs, but for the company with a do-it-yourself tradition, this book outlines the step-by-step procedure of evaluating the existing plan and, if necessary, creating a new one.

2
HISTORY AND CURRENT TRENDS

One of America's earliest hatters started in business by putting his day's output in a basket, putting the basketful of hats on his arm, and selling his product door to door. As his reputation grew, he sometimes got orders for more (or different) hats than those in his basket. He employed a trusted associate to help with the selling so that the hatter could spend more time at his bench making hats.

Somewhere along the line the hatter found that his salesman worked harder if he received a modest commission on the hats he sold, rather than a meager daily wage. The salesman's earnings rose. He got a horse and buggy instead of carrying his wares in a basket. The hatter's shop was soon overloaded with orders, and he had to hire another worker at his bench.

The year was 1885. This true story is, in microcosm, how

sales incentive compensation came to the American hat-making industry. Hatters weren't the only ones; other companies in other industries were following the same pattern.

In Western Europe and most of the rest of what we call the "free world" the same trends could be seen, modified according to the industry and the customs of the country, and usually decades behind the American practices.

In some European countries the development of sales incentive compensation has been hastened by the presence of selling companies or concessionaires, many of them established to evade the value-added taxes, with nearly all the employees involved in selling being paid on a commission-only basis. The separation that thus grew up between those who produced and those who sold became—especially in Western Europe—the basis of certain other distinctions. Salespersons were not considered employees in some countries, and these distinctions still persist.

In the United States, such separateness continued for many generations to keep salespersons' salaries nominal even when their total incomes were more than adequate. Companies have only recently begun to give sales personnel the same fringe benefits as those given other employees.

In the recognized discipline of marketing, the experts have been slow to acknowledge that sales incentive compensation could be a factor influencing a company's marketing mix. Much of the pioneering work in the field has understandably been carried out in those industries where the role of personal sales ability is supremely important.

For years there were only occasional magazine articles on sales compensation. Serious attention can hardly be said to have been given the subject until the 1930s.

Experimentation, tinkering with commissions schedules,

and other features of early sales incentive plans have, of course, been going on for years. Most of this experimentation was initiated by the sales executives themselves.

The only guideposts were a few articles, and books such as *Methods of Paying Salesmen and Operation Expenses in the Wholesale Grocery Industry* (Harvard Bureau of Business Research, 1918), *Tested Sales Compensation Plans* (*Printers' Ink*, 1937), and occasional references to compensation plans in publications of The Conference Board, the American Management Association, Dartnell Corporation, the Metropolitan Life Insurance Company Policy Codes Bureau, *Sales and Marketing Management* magazine, and the like.

REASONS FOR INCREASING INTEREST

Several developments during the past decade have converged to bring sales incentive compensation into much sharper focus and have greatly accelerated development in the field. Some of these influences were:

1. The shortcomings developed in many older plans during the sustained sellers' market conditions after World War II, especially during the 1960s

2. The recognition (belated in many cases) that salespersons were also company *employees* and were just as entitled to fringe benefits and equitable salaries as other white-collar workers

3. The growing recognition that the salesperson's job did not lend itself to being closely supervised, and that some motivating devices were clearly needed

4. The experience of companies under various federal

income control programs, under which salaries and frequently incentive compensation as well were frozen unless there were previously established brackets and established incentive plans

5. The ever-intensifying pressure for profits, which stimulated consideration of the idea that sales incentive compensation might contribute to them

6. The impact of inflation, especially the inflation-recession cycles of the 1970s.

MARKETING AND MANAGEMENT TRENDS

Interest in effective sales compensation plans has also been heightened by certain trends in management and marketing methods since World War II, among them:

1. The widespread adoption of the management-by-objectives philosophy created an atmosphere in which it was only logical to reward the achievement of sales objectives.

2. There has been increased stress on internal corporate communications, especially the communication of objectives and performance standards; these are an important function of any sales compensation plan.

3. Incentive compensation helps make selling costs more flexible—low when sales are low, high when sales are high. Only companies paying on a straight commission basis can achieve almost absolute flexibility of selling costs: no sales = no commission = few or no sales costs. But other types of incentive pay tended to pay well when sales were high, and less

well when sales were low. This had a strong appeal to many slenderly financed companies, as well as to many with adequate finances.

4. Good incentive plans do attract and hold good sales personnel, attracting some to selling as a career who might otherwise have looked elsewhere. An increasing number of company presidents come up through the sales ranks.

5. Not all sales reps by any means have a thick skin and an irrepressible store of self-motivation. Successive turndowns can erode the motivation of almost anyone, but a good incentive plan helps the sales reps pick themselves up and keep going.

6. The doctrine has spread, from General Motors down to far humbler enterprises, that profits can be boosted by incentives not only at the executive level, but also at the sales force level.

7. There has been increasing acceptance of the validity of the reason some companies adopted compensation plans decades ago: namely, they help improve supervision.

8. Finally, some managements have probably been induced to adopt incentive programs to head off the threat of unionization of their sales forces. While sales reps' unions have not become widespread, most driver-salespersons are unionized, as are many sales reps in such fields as automobiles, newspaper circulation, insurance, real estate, utilities, liquor, and clothing. Although unions among field sales personnel may not spread much further than at present,

their existence is doubtless closely related to compensation, and union drives have undoubtedly spurred
some adoptions of sales incentives compensation.

RECENT TRENDS

Over the past half century there has been a steady growth in the
percentage of companies using some kind of sales incentive
program combining a guaranteed salary with an extra incentive
payment for superior performance.

Some definitions are in order. In a *straight salary* program,
sales representatives receive a fixed salary. Superior performance
can be rewarded with a salary increase, but there is no
immediate relationship between sales results and earnings.

In a *straight commission* plan, the sales representive usually
receives a fixed percentage of the dollar value of goods sold. The
commission may vary from one line to another; it may be paid
when the product is sold, shipped, or paid for; it may vary from
as little as 2 percent to as much as 40 or 50 percent in some
forms of direct selling. The straight commission sales rep often
pays his or her own expenses.

In a *draw-against-commission* plan, the company simply
advances, or lends, the sales rep some "living money," which
the rep is expected to repay out of future commissions. The draw
can be large enough to resemble a salary-plus-commission
arrangement. The difference is that if the commissions earned
on a drawing account basis are less than the amount of the draw,
the salesperson theoretically owes the company the difference;
the salary-plus-commission rep usually does not assume any
liability for the deficit. In practice, it is often necessary to write
off an accumulated deficit if the company wishes to keep the
sales rep.

In a *salary-plus-incentive* program, the salesperson receives a base salary which is usually large enough to cover his or her living expenses, plus additional payment based on sales results. The incentive portion of the sales rep's pay will be referred to as *commission* if it is directly and arithmetically related to the dollar amounts sold; it will be called a *bonus* if it is based on other factors such as company profits, performance evaluation, or the attainment of specified objectives. In either case, the incentive may be based on the sales rep's individual performance, or upon the pooled accomplishments of a group of salespersons.

The word *guarantee* will be used to refer to that fixed portion of the sales rep's income which is received regardless of accomplishments. The *contingency amount* or *incentive payment* refers to additional payments based on results.

For half a century, the percentage of salespersons paid a salary plus some kind of incentive has been increasing, although it appears to have leveled off recently. Straight salary and straight commission are the two plans which have been losing ground, with commission plans much the heavier loser. A recent questionnaire by the authors, described in more detail in Chapter 4, revealed the following pattern:

- About 15 percent of the companies were paying their salespersons straight salary.

- About 15 percent were paying their sales reps straight commission.

- About 10 percent were advancing a draw against commission.

- Nearly 60 percent were paying salary plus incentive payments.

3

WHAT A GOOD COMPENSATION PLAN CAN AND CANNOT DO

The designer of an incentive compensation plan is doomed to disappointment if the plan is expected to perform miracles or to overcome weaknesses in other functions of the company.

WHAT A GOOD PLAN CAN DO

1. *A good sales incentive plan can increase company profits by motivating the sales force to allocate its time and efforts in a way that maximizes profits.* Ordinarily, management has some idea as to how the sales force should perform to help attain corporate profit objectives. It can lay down guidelines on such functions as:

- How to analyze the potential market and plan the local coverage necessary to achieve sales targets

- How to allocate selling time among product lines and market segments, among types and sizes of customers, among present and prospective customers

- How to handle inquiries, make presentations on products or services, overcome objections or complaints, and close the sale

- How to handle any after-the-sale responsibilities, what service work to do and not to do, how to build customer good will

- In short, how to organize the work

But it is one thing to lay down guidelines, and another to make sure that the sales rep, operating out in the field, actually follows them. A good incentive plan should be tailored to encourage the performance of these duties and discourage unproductive omissions or shortcuts. This, as a rule, is not a difficult requirement to meet, since it is the main objective of the compensation plan.

2. *A good plan can motivate the sales force throughout the year, and not simply at quota times.* Many plans fall short in this respect. Two ways to meet this objective are:

- Keep the quota periods as short as possible within the industry selling cycle and without increasing administrative expense unreasonably.

Pay out frequently and promptly, again within the limits of the selling cycle and administrative efficiency. A prompt reward motivates vastly better than a delayed reward of equal size, but payment should not be so frequent that the amounts paid seem insignificant—strive for balance. If payment is relatively infrequent, motivation can be sustained by frequent reports on the amount of unpaid incentive accumulated to date.

3. *A good plan can emphasize profits, so that the sales reps who generate the greatest profits receive the greatest rewards.* There has been much discussion pro and con on this point.

   Some managements don't want the sales force to know the margin of profit on various products, fearing that it will look large to them and thus tempt them to cut prices. The answer to this, of course, is to provide a higher payoff on the more profitable products without giving specific data on margins or profits.

   Some managements even hesitate to tell their sales reps which products command the best gross profits—but these, fortunately, are in the minority.

   In general, wherever the profit on a sale or a territory depends importantly upon the product mix sold, this requirement can usually be met, and the plan designer should try to meet it. The only exceptions are those situations in which a higher bonus on the more profitable products might produce inequities, as would be the case if the potential market for these products exists in only a few territories. Even in these cases there are ways to deal with the problem. This subject will be discussed in detail later.

4. *A good plan can reduce undesirable turnover.* The most capable sales reps are the ones most likely to be lured away if a competitor's compensation offers them greater rewards for their productivity. By keeping each rep's total pay in line with accomplishments, much of this attrition can be prevented.

   Conversely, because a good plan measures and rewards individual productivity, it becomes easier to identify and get rid of the incompetents—if, indeed, their lack of earnings under an incentive plan does not cause them to leave voluntarily.

5. *A good plan can be administered without burdensome costs.* This is a question of trade-offs. If some increase in the complexity or administrative expense of a plan will produce gratifying increases in profits, this increase might be warranted.

6. *A good plan can be simple—if necessary.* A couple of decades ago, it was commonly believed that simplicity—ease of understanding on the part of the sales force—was the paramount requirement for an effective sales compensation plan. The authors, having seen many plans that were extremely effective even though they required many pages of explanation, would qualify this. Simplicity is always a desirable factor. But where incentive earning opportunities are substantial, and where the sales job requires a high level of intelligence, knowledge, and

skill, simplicity may be less important. Where these conditions are not present, simplicity continues to be not only desirable, but practically imperative.

WHAT NO SALES INCENTIVE PLAN CAN DO

1. *A compensation plan can never take the place of active direction and control by management.* Picture a company whose sales reps are on a straight salary. The sales manager is frustrated because they spend too much time with small customers, don't do enough prospecting, and knock off early on Fridays ("customers don't want to see you then, anyway").

   Eureka! He puts them on an incentive program. *Now,* knowing that their income is directly dependent upon sales volume, *now* they'll do all those things the sales manager has been telling them to do for years. So what happens? Sales reps continue to spend too much time with small customers, don't do enough prospecting, and knock off early on Fridays.

   People don't suddenly become logical, superefficient machines just because they are offered a reward for productivity. A sales incentive plan is an aid to management, but can never take the place of active direction and control by management. There will always be the need for a manager's hardnosed analysis of individual performance and development of programs for individual sales reps.

2. *A compensation plan cannot be the sole motivator of top performance.* The incentive program is just one factor in the motivational pattern, albeit one of the

most important ones. Every sales rep is still motivated, in varying degrees to be sure, by such nonfinancial factors as:

- Respect for one's company, its products, and its managers

- A feeling of accomplishment generated by attaining objectives which he or she has helped to set

3. A *good sales incentive plan should offer the job enrichment factors defined by Herzberg:**

- Some voice in how the job is to be handled, a feeling that one is developing innate skills and abilities

- The feeling that the company, and the immediate boss, recognize the rep's existence and importance, respect the rep, and listen to him or her

- The conviction that he or she has a future with the company

- Pride in his or her own abilities as a salesperson

4. A *sales incentive plan cannot continue to be effective:*

- If the marketing conditions it was designed to meet have changed significantly.

- If the plan is not well administered. More than one plan, while inherently good, has failed to work because sales quotas were unrealistic, results were

---

*Frederick Herzberg, Bernard Mausner, and B. Synderman, *The Motivation to Work*, John Wiley & Sons, Inc., New York, 1959.

not reported accurately and reasonably promptly, or it was poorly administered in other basic respects.

• If the balance between a guaranteed income and contingent income is radically changed. More about this later.

A note of caution: Are sales incentive compensation plans appropriate for all marketers? No. There are situations where sales incentive compensation plans should probably be avoided. Most of these situations fall into three major categories:

1. Where the administration of a good incentive plan would probably present impossibly cumbersome problems

2. Where marketing management can keep motivation high without any such plan

3. Where it is impossible to measure the contribution of the individual salesperson, or even of the sales force as a whole

   The role of airline sales reps who call on travel agencies is an example. What direct correlation can be shown between the quantity or quality of a rep's calls on an agency and the number of passengers boarding the rep's airline?

4

WHO USES WHAT, AND WHY

What percentages of American companies are using each of the four types of compensation plans, and how satisfied are they with them? What, based on their own experiences, are the advantages and disadvantages of each type of plan?

To answer those questions the authors, with the cooperation of *Sales and Marketing Management* magazine, mailed a questionnaire to 3,000 sales executives. Replies were received from 449—a 15 percent response, indicating the degree of interest in this subject.

Table 4-1 shows, for three basic types of businesses, the percentage using each plan, and the percentage of users satisfied or dissatisfied with the plan. (Retail compensation plans are treated separately in Chapter 23.)

Plans involving a base salary plus some form of incentive are used by more companies than all other types of plans combined. Straight salary plans were second most popular in manufacturing and service industries, while some form of commission plan was second most popular among wholesalers and distributors.

About 75 percent of those using commission plans were satisfied with their plans, as compared with 65.2 percent

TABLE 4-1 Plans in Use

Type of plan	% using it	Percentage of users		No answer or no opinion
		Satisfied	Dissatisfied	
MANUFACTURERS				
Salary + incentive	59.8	60.5	36.1	3.4
Straight salary	15.0	45.9	43.3	10.8
Straight commission	14.6	80.6	8.3	11.1
Draw vs. commission	10.6	80.8	19.2	
WHOLESALERS, DISTRIBUTORS, MANUFACTURERS' REPS				
Salary + incentive	53.9	74.7	22.7	2.6
Straight salary	6.5	55.6*	44.4*	
Straight commission	15.8	72.7	18.2	9.1
Draw vs. commission	23.8	63.6	30.3	6.1
SERVICE INDUSTRIES				
Salary + incentive	58.1	64.0	36.0	
Straight salary	25.6	36.4	63.6	
Straight commission	9.3	75.0*	25.0*	
Draw vs. commission	7.0	100.0*		
TOTALS, ALL RESPONDENTS				
Salary + incentive	57.7	65.2	32.0	2.8
Straight salary	13.3	45.6	47.4	7.0
Straight commission	14.5	77.4	12.9	9.7
Draw vs. commission	14.5	72.6	24.2	3.2
Total	100.0	65.8	30.5	4.4

*Percentage represents a breakdown of 10 or fewer respondents.

satisfied with salary-plus-incentive plans and only 45 percent with straight salary plans.

It is surprising that more than one-third of the responding companies were either dissatisfied with their plans or undecided about their merits. If their present plans are so disappointing, why didn't they do something about them long ago? The answers probably are:

1. Entrenched industry traditions, which are difficult to buck

2. Difficulty in assigning credit for a sale when various salespersons, sales offices, and company departments participate in the selling function

3. Complicated financial or product-line considerations

4. Lack of realization that an appropriate plan can enhance profits

This last point is corroborated by an analysis of the bases used for calculating commissions or incentive pay by companies using that type of compensation (Table 4-2).

In most companies handling multiple products or services, profitability varies greatly from one to another, and the more profitable products usually require more time and effort to sell. If the sales force is paid on the basis of dollar volume, they will tend to push the low-profit, easy-to-sell items instead of concentrating on the more profitable ones. Yet total dollar volume was by far the most widely used basis for calculating commissions or incentive payments.

TABLE 4-2 Basis of Calculating Commissions or Incentive Payments

Basis used	% of companies using it
Total dollar volume	42.7
Dollar volume by product line	10.3
Units sold	2.7
Total gross margin	10.3
Gross margin by product line	2.3
Contribution to profit	5.3
Weighted units	4.6
Judgment	0.8
Combination of two or more of these	21.0
	100.0

Even more astonishing was the answer to this question: "If you are not now doing it, have you considered using some type of incentive plan that would enhance the average profitability of the products sold?"

The answers were:

	Yes	No
Those dissatisfied with present plans	72.2%	27.8%
Those satisfied with present plans	59.5%	40.8%
Total all respondents	64.0%	36.0%

One-third of all respondents have never seriously asked themselves if some change in their compensation plan could increase profits rather than volume!

"Is your incentive plan based on a quota?" Yes, said 64.9 percent; no, 35.1 percent.

"How often are incentive payments made?" The answers:

Weekly	0.6%
Biweekly	1.2%
Monthly	1.0%
Quarterly	52.0%
Semiannually	5.8%
Annually	27.2%
As earned	2.3%

"When does the salesperson get credit for the sale?"

When booked	11.9%
When shipped or invoiced	64.3%
When paid for	22.5%
Part at one time, part at another	1.3%

What do users view as the principal advantages and disadvantages of the plans they are using? Answers to that question appear in Tables 4-3 to 4-6. The first figure after each citation is the number of respondents mentioning that advantage or disadvantage; the second is each factor's percentage of the total number of factors mentioned. For example, if 100 respondents mentioned a total of 150 advantages, and 15 cited the same advantage, that would represent 10 percent of total citations.

Some of these reactions deserve comment.

TABLE 4-3   Advantages and Disadvantages of Salary-Plus-Incentive Plans

Advantages cited	Respondents	Percentage	Disadvantages cited	Respondents	Percentage
Motivates greater effort	46	16.8	Incentive not large enough to motivate; cap on earnings	37	17.7
Increased earnings for sales force	38	13.4	No disadvantages	21	10.0
Increased sales, profits	21	7.6	Fluctuations in income	18	8.6
Simple, easy to administer	21	7.6	Incentives not related to margins or profits	15	7.2
Pay is related to performance	18	6.5	Difficulty in setting fair quotas	12	5.7
Balance between security and incentive	16	5.8	Complexity, administrative costs	12	5.7
Aids recruiting, reduces turnover	11	4.0	High sales costs as volume increases	9	4.3
Control of selling costs	10	3.6	Unfair territory differences	5	2.4
High-margin items stressed	10	3.6	Incentive payments not frequent enough	4	1.9
Security; income in bad times	10	3.6	Salespersons not compensated for some of their efforts	4	1.9
Recognition for high performance	9	3.3			

Control, manager can require nonselling chores	9	3.3	Company advances incentive before collecting	4	1.9
Measurement of performance	8	2.9	Not based 100% on individual performance	3	1.4
Promotes teamwork	6	2.2	Difficulty in recruiting	2	1.0
Fair to both sides	4	1.4	Underachievers sometimes overpaid	2	1.0
Morale and enthusiasm	2	0.7	Incentive arbitrarily determined	2	1.0
Encourages full-line selling	2	0.7	Sometimes difficult to direct efforts	2	1.0
All others, one mention each	36	13.0	Loss of money advanced to salespersons who fail	2	1.0
			All others, one mention each	55	26.3

TABLE 4-4 Advantages and Disadvantages of Straight Salary Plans

Advantages cited	Respondents	Percentage	Disadvantages cited	Respondents	Percentage
Security; steady income	23	38.3	Lack of motivation of sales force	30	57.7
Simple, easy to administer	9	15.0	No disadvantages	6	11.5
Fixed selling expense	5	8.3	Salespersons' income limited	3	5.8
Control over sales force	5	8.3	No goals, yardsticks	3	5.8
Makes recruiting easier	2	3.3	Inflexible	2	3.8
None	2	3.3	All others, one each	8	15.4
All others, one mention each	14	23.3			

TABLE 4-5 Advantages and Disadvantages of Straight Commission Plans

Advantages cited	Respondents	Percentage	Disadvantages cited	Respondents	Percentage
High earnings for sales force	24	34.3	Uncertain, fluctuating income	13	23.2
Known cost ratio, lower dollar costs when sales are down	14	20.0	Lack of control	13	23.2
Sales force motivated	12	17.1	Salespersons take on other lines	5	8.9
Company pays only for results	8	11.4	No disadvantages	4	7.1
Increases profits	2	2.9	Difficulty in recruiting	4	7.1
Simple	2	2.9	Difficulty in starting new rep	3	5.2
All others, one mention each	8	11.4	Poor salespersons starve	3	5.2
			Higher turnover	2	3.6
			All others, one mention each	9	16.1

TABLE 4-6 Advantages and Disadvantages of Draw-Against-Commission Plans

Advantages cited	Respondents	Percentage	Disadvantages cited	Respondents	Percentage
Motivated sales force	20	23.8	No disadvantages	10	17.4
High earnings for sales force	17	20.2	Insecurity, uncertain income	8	14.0
Simple, easy to administer	9	10.7	Lack of control over sales force	5	8.8
Known cost ratio, lower dollar costs with low sales	8	9.5	Inequities in territory potential	5	8.8
Company pays only for results	4	4.8	Inflationary increases in expenses paid by salespersons	3	5.3
Draw provides some security	3	3.6			
Minimizes sales costs	2	2.4	Difficulty in developing new salespersons	3	5.3
Increases volume, profits	2	2.4	Sales force skims markets, sells mainly the "hot" items	3	5.3
Attracts aggressive salespersons	2	2.4			
Sales force is profit-minded	2	2.4	Complicated commission schedule	2	3.5
All others, one mention each	15	17.8	Difficulty in recruiting	2	3.5
			All others, one mention each	16	28.1

SALARY-PLUS-INCENTIVE PLANS

It is noteworthy that 12 respondents said their plans promoted the sale of profitable items or encouraged full-line selling. This is true only of plans designed with these objectives in mind—an incentive based on dollar volume alone tends to encourage emphasis on the products easiest to sell.

The disadvantage most frequently cited was offering incentive payments too low to motivate the sales force to additional effort. This was cited by most of those dissatisfied with their salary-plus-incentive plans, but was also recognized as a disadvantage by many who were satisfied with their plan.

With inflation pushing income into higher tax brackets and reducing purchasing power, an incentive which was adequate a few years ago simply does not motivate the sales force today. And, as one respondent pointed out, incentive payments that don't produce results are "simply an added expense." Notice, too, the number of respondents who were unhappy because incentive payments were not related to the profitability of the products sold.

STRAIGHT SALARY

The outstanding finding here is the very high percentage of respondents reporting that salespersons on a straight salary are simply not motivated. "Lack of incentive" represented 57.7 percent of all disadvantages cited, a far higher percentage than that listed for any other advantage or disadvantage of any type of plan. It was recognized as a disadvantage by those satisfied with their salary plans as well as those dissatisfied with them.

COMMISSION PLANS

The major advantages of both straight commission and draw-against-commission plans are a highly motivated sales force as a result of virtually unlimited earnings, and sales costs that decrease when sales decrease. The latter factor is more frequently mentioned by those paying straight commission than by those providing a draw.

Although many users of both plans reported that they saw no disadvantages in them, those who did cite disadvantages most frequently mentioned the uncertain income to the salespersons and the lack of control over the sales force.

TWO

PRELIMINARIES

5

ESTABLISHING
THE OBJECTIVES

Clarity of objectives is fundamental in designing an effective compensation plan. The plan should be targeted toward one key strategic objective; any other desired outcomes of the plan should be considered as subsidiary or "housekeeping" objectives.

The key objective might be, for example, to increase sales volume with the existing product mix. The company might also want salespersons to open new accounts, concentrate on the more profitable customers, run dealer meetings and report market conditions—but these should not ordinarily be considered proper objectives of the plan. They are the tactics which management will develop in the sales force to help it in attaining the key objective—*volume.*

The plan designer should, at all costs, resist the temptation to incorporate too many objectives, heeding the desires of every sales executive he consults. A survey by the Conference Board in the early 1970s* showed a tendency for the effectiveness of incentive compensation plans to diminish as the number of objectives increased. Two or perhaps three objectives provided the optimal results.

Some 21 percent of the respondents to the authors' current survey indicated that they used combinations of various factors in determining incentive payments. It is interesting to note that only 50 percent of these companies were satisfied with their compensation plans, compared with 64.7 percent of those which based incentive payments purely on dollar volume sold.

STRATEGIC OBJECTIVES

Lists of possible strategic objectives from which one or two key objectives might be selected often look something like this:

1. To increase the company's return on investment

2. To increase sales volume:

    a. Across the board

    b. Primarily in certain profitable products (improved product mix)

3. To increase profits:

    a. As a dollar amount

    b. As a percentage of sales

4. To increase market share

*National Industrial Conference Board, *Studies in Personnel Policy*, no. 217.

5. To make the company more competitive in the marketplace

But analysis will indicate that these potential objectives are not mutually exclusive.

Every company wants to increase its return on investment (ROI), but how? Can it be most easily accomplished by a drive for greater sales volume with the present product mix? Or could ROI most easily be increased by selling a higher percentage of the more profitable products? Or is the answer some blend of X percent increase in total volume and Y percent improvement in the product mix?

Increase in sales volume is a clear enough objective. But it is important to determine whether the goal is increased volume with the present product mix, or increased volume in the profitable products, which represents an improvement in product mix.

An increase in the total dollars of profit might be achieved by either a volume increase, an improvement in the product mix, or some blend of the two. Increase in profits as a percentage of sales can be achieved primarily by improving the product mix, although an across-the-board increase in volume would tend to reduce the percentage of overhead costs and thus improve the profit percentage.

If the goal is to increase market share or to make the company more competitive, these can probably be attained by emphasizing total volume. A company might be willing to reduce its immediate profits in order to attain either of these objectives, feeling that a larger share of market would enable it to reap larger profits and show a better ROI in the future.

What this adds up to is that the compensation plan designer must get agreement on *one* of these as the key objective of the plan:

1. Increase sales volume across the board if one is relatively satisfied with the present product mix.

2. Improve the product mix, with any resulting increase in total sales as a by-product.

3. Achieve an X percent increase in total volume accompanied by a Y percent improvement in product mix.

If this determination is carefully made and constantly kept in mind, it will serve as a guideline while developing details of the compensation plan.

TACTICAL OBJECTIVES

Given the key strategic objective, how can the plan assist in its attainment? To succeed, the compensation plan will need to do most of the following (although some may not be applicable in particular cases):

1. Motivate the sales force. This is a must.

2. Be competitive with compensation plans which may lure sales reps away.

3. Be fair to both the sales force and the company.

4. Reinforce successful sales habits or behavior patterns on the part of the sales force.

5. Provide for stability of sales.

6. Reduce or control the sales/expense ratio.

7. Be flexible with respect to the following:

a. Apply to missionary territories as well as established territories.

b. Provide for changes in territories.

c. Provide for changes in the size or character of the sales force.

d. Provide for changes in product emphasis.

e. Be effective in recessions as well as booms.

f. Avoid the necessity of frequent changes.

8. Make it possible to recruit, train, and retain the desired type of sales personnel. Building loyalty and morale, sometimes cited as a possible objective, is a subordinate objective in reducing turnover.

OBJECTIVES INVOLVING BEHAVIORAL CHANGE

The compensation plan, if it is to achieve its key objective, must encourage the sales force to perform in an effective way. These desired work habits might include such activities as prospecting, running dealer or distributor meetings, doing promotional work, minimizing expenses, and so on.

It is a mistake to consider some of these as objectives of the compensation plan and attempt to provide specific rewards for them. It is the task of sales management to convince the salesperson that these are the routes to the maximum incentive earnings.

These behavioral objectives are worth listing, however, as a checklist to assure the designer that his or her proposed plan is compatible with the desired work habits, and above all does not penalize or discourage a desired activity.

The plan, then, should ultimately reward the salesperson who does whichever of these are applicable to the company:

1. Stresses the most profitable products

2. Concentrates on the most profitable customers

3. Does across-the-line selling

4. Performs supporting or nonselling tasks such as promotion, missionary work, and customer service

5. Cooperates with other salespersons, other levels of the sales force, and other company departments

6. Keeps headquarters informed of his or her own activities and of market conditions

7. Makes effective sales calls, using the best applicable professional techniques

8. Allocates his or her time among large and small customers, among customers and prospects, among products, among selling and nonselling functions, in such a way as to maximize results

9. Applies appropriate selling efforts during all seasons

OPERATIONAL OBJECTIVES

If the sales plan is to function smoothly, certain operational objectives must be met. Among those possible are:

1. It should be reasonably clear and easy to understand.

2. It should not require excessive administrative costs.

3. It should eliminate frequent discussions or arguments about compensation.

OBJECTIVES OF THE SALES PERSONNEL

Finally, if the compensation plan is to motivate salespersons to do what the company wants, the plan should give salespersons as much as possible of what *they* want.

Here are some of the sales force objectives to keep in mind:

1. Potential after-tax incentive payments large enough to justify the extra effort

2. Incentive payments reasonably frequent and prompt

3. Where applicable, a good balance between security (base pay) and incentive

4. Rewards based on individual performance, and only on factors under the salesperson's control

5. Income that does not fluctuate greatly when the salesperson is performing consistently

6. No ceiling on earnings under normal conditions

7. Compensation commensurate with sales results

8. Opportunity for advancement without financial loss

9. Incentives based on clear measurements of accomplishment, without arbitrary factors

10. Salesperson not unduly penalized by inaccuracies in establishing quotas

11. Salesperson not unduly penalized by differences in potential of assigned territories or accounts

Although this chapter has listed 36 possible subordinate objectives to be considered in addition to the key aim, it is usually not too difficult to meet most of these goals while keeping one's eye on the main one.

6

EVALUATING AN EXISTING PLAN

Only after major and minor objectives have been agreed upon is it possible to evaluate an existing plan. Once the objectives are clear, one simply needs to ask, "What is the relative importance of each objective, and how well is our compensation plan helping to attain each?"

Table 6-1 is a checklist that will be useful in analyzing an existing plan. Basically, you give each objective a weighting as to its importance and a rating as to how well it is being supported by the present plan; you then multiply the weight by the rating to get a score on each. The total of these scores for individual objectives is a rough numerical evaluation of the plan.

The authors have arbitrarily assigned the heaviest range of weights to the three possible key strategic objectives, second heaviest range to motivating the sales force and providing

Example: Rating Checklist

Objective	Weight	Rating	Score Unimportant	Score Rated
TACTICAL				
Motivate sales force	x +5 +10 (+15)	−2 0 (+2) +4	40	(30)
Match competitors' plans	(x) +1 +2 +3	−2 0 +2 +4	(8)	
Fair to company and sales force	x +1 (+2) +3	−2 0 +2 (+4)	8	(8)
		Total, these three objectives:	8	38
		Grand total:	46	

adequate incentive payments, and an equal range of weights to all the others.

It would not be logical to assign a zero rating to an objective which is not applicable; this would give the lowest ratings to plans with the smallest number of objectives, just the opposite of our recommendations. Therefore, the form is designed to give an average score to any objectives not relevant to the specific sales force.

To use the form, consider each of the listed objectives and ask yourself two questions: "How important is this objective to my company?" and "How well is our compensation plan helping us to attain this objective?" (See example, page 48.)

Use the columns headed "Weight" to indicate how important each objective is to your company. If it is unimportant, or not applicable, circle the "x" opposite the objective. If it is slightly important, very important, or critical, circle the number under the appropriate column heading. Note that you are instructed to give a weight to just one of the three possible strategic objectives, circling the "x" for the other two.

Use the columns headed "Rating" to indicate how well your plan is helping to attain each objective. If you marked the objective with an "x" for unimportant, ignore the ratings. But if you gave the objective any positive weight, decide whether your plan is hindering the attainment of the objective, having no effect upon it, helping some, or helping a great deal. For each objective, circle the number under the appropriate heading.

Now, in the two colums headed "Score":

1. If you gave an objective a weight of "x" for unimportant, circle the number opposite that objective in the left-hand score column, headed "Unimportant."

2. If you gave that objective any other weight, multiply your weight for that objective by your rating for that objective, and enter the result in the right-hand score column.

There is, unfortunately, no established "par" enabling you to compare the rating of your plan with ratings of others in your industry. You can, however, use this method to compare your plan with a competitor's plan with which you are familiar, or to compare two tentative versions of a plan you are designing. In any event, Table 6-1 will serve as a useful checklist and reminder.

GETTING INFORMATION ON COMPETITORS

One of the most important factors to consider in evaluating an existing or proposed sales incentive compensation plan is how it compares with those offered by competitors. A company need not offer its sales force exactly the same pay schedule its competitors offer theirs, but it is courting trouble if the total income levels its package provide do not at least approximate those prevailing in the industry.

Most well-managed companies are alert to this problem, getting their intelligence through their own sales force, through purchased surveys or services, or through the activities of their own industrial relations departments.

The designer of the sales compensation plan needs to know, for the sales forces of similar companies:

1. What was the minimum, median, and maximum *guaranteed salary* for the most recent complete year?

TABLE 6-1 Rating Your Compensation Plan

Objective	Weight (How important is this objective to your company? Circle one.)				Rating (Multiply the weight by this number. In meeting each objective does your plan—)				Score	
	Unimportant or not applicable	Slightly Important	Very Important	Critical	Hinder?	Have no effect?	Help some?	Help much?	Unimportant or not applicable; give your plan	Rated objectives; weight times rating
STRATEGIC (Select just one strategic objective; circle the "x" after the other two.)										
(1) Increased volume	x	+10	+20	+30	−2	0	+2	+4	80	
(2) More profitable product mix	x	+10	+20	+30	−2	0	+2	+4	80	
(3) Balance between 1 and 2	x	+10	+20	+30	−2	0	+2	+4	80	
TACTICAL										
(1) Motivate sales force	x	+5	+10	+15	−2	0	+2	+4	40	
(2) Match competitors' plans	x	+1	+2	+3	−2	0	+2	+4	8	
(3) Fair to both company and sales force	x	+1	+2	+3	−2	0	+2	+4	8	
(4) Reinforce desired work patterns	x	+1	+2	+3	−2	0	+2	+4	8	

TABLE 6-1 Rating Your Compensation Plan (continued)

Objective	Weight (How important is this objective to your company? Circle one.)				Rating (Multiply the weight by this number.) In meeting each objective does your plan—				Score	
	Unimportant or not applicable	Slightly important	Very important	Critical	Hinder?	Have no effect?	Help some?	Help much?	Unimportant or not applicable; give your plan	Rated objectives; weight times rating
(5) Promote stability in sales	×	+ 1	+ 2	+ 3	− 2	0	+ 2	+ 4	80	
(6) Reduce or control expenses	×	+ 1	+ 2	+ 3	− 2	0	+ 2	+ 4		
(7) Flexible as to changes in territories, products	×	+ 1	+ 2	+ 3	− 2	0	+ 2	+ 4	8	
(8) Aid in recruiting and retaining people	×	+ 1	+ 2	+ 3	− 2	0	+ 2	+ 4	8	
BEHAVIORAL CHANGES										
(1) Stress profitable products	×	+ 1	+ 2	+ 3	− 2	0	+ 2	+ 4	8	
(2) Concentrate on most profitable customers	×	+ 1	+ 2	+ 3	− 2	0	+ 2	+ 4	8	
(3) Promote across-the-line selling	×	+ 1	+ 2	+ 3	− 2	0	+ 2	+ 4	8	
(4) Encourage nonselling functions; provide control of sales force	×	+ 1	+ 2	+ 3	− 2	0	+ 2	+ 4	8	
(5) Promote cooperation	×	+ 1	+ 2	+ 3	− 2	0	+ 2	+ 4	8	

(6) Encourage communication with headquarters	x	+1	+2	+3	−2	0	+2	+4	8
(7) Encourage effective sales calls	x	+1	+2	+3	−2	0	+2	+4	8
(8) Encourage effective allocation of time	x	+1	+2	+3	−2	0	+2	+4	
(9) Encourage year-round sales efforts	x	+1	+2	+3	−2	0	+2	+4	8
OPERATIONAL									
(1) Clear, simple	x	+1	+2	+3	−2	0	+2	+4	8
(2) Reasonably easy to administer	x	+1	+2	+3	−2	0	+2	+4	8
(3) Ends arguments about compensation	x	+1	+2	+3	−2	0	+2	+4	8
SALES FORCE WANTS									
(1) Adequate size of incentives	x	+5	+10	+15	−2	0	+2	+4	40
(2) Frequent payment	x	+1	+2	+3	−2	0	+2	+4	8
(3) Balance between security, incentive	x	+1	+2	+3	−2	0	+2	+4	8
(4) Rewards individual performance	x	+1	+2	+3	−2	0	+2	+4	8
(5) Avoids unmerited fluctuations in income	x	+1	+2	+3	−2	0	+2	+4	8
(6) Avoids ceilings under normal conditions	x	+1	+2	+3	−2	0	+2	+4	8

TABLE 6-1 Rating Your Compensation Plan *(continued)*

Objective	Weight (How important is this objective to your company? Circle one.)				Rating (Multiply the weight by this number.) In meeting each objective does your plan—				Score	
	Unimportant or not applicable	Slightly Important	Very Important	Critical	Hinder?	Have no effect?	Help some?	Help much?	Unimportant or not applicable; give your plan	Rated objectives; weight times rating
(7) Compensation is commensurate with sales results	x	+1	+2	+3	-2	0	+2	+4	8	
(8) Opportunity for promotion without financial losses	x	+1	+2	+3	-2	0	+2	+4	8	
(9) Clear measurement	x	+1	+2	+3	-2	0	+2	+4	8	
(10) Salesperson not unduly penalized if quota is inaccurate	x	+1	+2	+3	-2	0	+2	+4	8	
(11) Salesperson not unduly penalized by differences in potential	x	+1	+2	+3	-2	0	+2	+4	8	
					Total, these three objectives:					
								Grand total:		

2. What was the minimum, median, and maximum amount of incentive pay?

3. What was the minimum, median, and maximum total income?

4. What was the pay arrangement for beginning sales reps?

Organizations such as the American Management Association make available annual surveys of sales compensation by industry. A difficulty with such surveys is that the user can't be sure that the income statistics apply to sales forces whose functions and problems are similar to his or her own. Selling standardized industrial chemicals by the carload is a far different job from selling a new specialty chemical that requires considerable missionary work and technical service, although in most surveys data on both compensation plans would be lumped together under "chemical industry." It is of no great value to a sales manager selling electric trains to obtain income figures for the toy industry, which includes salespersons selling everything from yo-yos to stuffed animals. The figures needed are those for sales forces selling competitive products through the same channels of distribution—the competing sales reps that the manager's own sales force meet head-to-head every day in their territories.

As consultants, the authors find it easy to telephone the personnel departments of competing companies, explaining that they are making a survey of sales compensation levels and offering to send a copy of the results, without identifying companies, to every cooperating company. "You will receive exactly the same information our client will get," the competitor is told. And the competitor does.

If the company's own compensation analyst or personnel department is making the survey, it is sometimes easier to get the information if competitors are asked to send their statistics to the inquiring company's auditing firm. Many industrial relations departments make yearly surveys of competitive pay plans as a matter of routine.

7

ANALYZING PRODUCT LINE PROFITABILITY

The old recipe for rabbit stew begins, "First, catch a rabbit." The recipe for a sales incentive compensation plan that will maximize profits begins: "First, be sure you know where the profits are." For any manufacturer, wholesaler, retailer, or service firm handling a mix of products or services, some items are usually much more profitable than others.

Profitability may not be directly related to the margin or markup on the product. When direct costs—selling, shipping, servicing, collecting—are deducted from the margin, the high markup product may contribute less to profits than one with a lower markup but lower marketing costs. For many companies, total profit is a combination of profits on some product lines, minus actual losses on others. Similarly, some types of customers are more profitable than others, some product sizes are more profitable than others, some sales territories yield more profit than others—even though the gross dollars may be the same in all cases.

Relative profitability of products and customers is determined by a method called "distribution cost analysis" or "product line profitability analysis." Readers whose companies regularly make this type of profit analysis are invited to skip this chapter. Those whose companies base their decisions primarily on sales dollars may find it the most important chapter in the book. It describes a rough-and-ready method of approximating relative profits.* Even this rough method, however, will yield surprising and important information.

As an example, we'll analyze the product line profitability of a manufacturer. Retailers, wholesalers and service firms should find it easy to apply the same basic method.

The analysis made by our hypothetical manufacturer is shown in Table 7-1. The firm makes four products:

- Product BB (for bread-and-butter) is an old product on which there is considerable price competition—hence the gross profit margin is only 30 percent of sales costs, compared with 40 and 50 percent for the others. However, product BB represents 50 percent of the firm's sales volume and top management frequently

---

*Those wishing to pursue this subject in greater depth are referred to Donald R. Longman and Michael Schiff, *Practical Distribution Cost Analysis*, Richard D. Irwin, Inc., 1955; Michael Schiff and Martin Mellman, *Financial Management of the Marketing Function*, Financial Executives Research Foundation, New York, 1962; John Barry, *Accounting's Role in Marketing*, Management Services, American Institute of CPA's, New York, 1967; "How to Pinpoint Marketing Problems," John Barry, Action Idea No. 44, Business Management Council Section of *Business Management* magazine, 22 West Putnam Avenue, Greenwich, Conn. 1965.

TABLE 7-1 Product Profitability Analysis of a Manufacturer
(in thousands)

	Product				
	BB	**SS**	**AV**	**NP**	**Total**
(1) Sales	$5,000	$2,500	$1,500	$1,000	$10,000
(2) % of total sales	50	25	15	10	100
(3) Manufacturing costs	$3,500	$1,500	$ 900	$ 500	$ 6,400
(4) Manufacturing costs as % of sales	70	60	60	50	
(5) Gross profit (1) − (3)	$1,500	$1,000	$ 600	$ 500	$ 3,600
DIRECT COSTS					
(6) Sales and sales management	$ 600	$ 150	$ 100	$ 150	$ 1,000
(7) Inventory	150	75	45	30	300
(8) Warehousing	125	30	30	15	200
(9) Billing and credit	120	25	35	20	200
(10) Shipping	55	15	20	10	100
(11) Advertising and promotion	100	25	25	50	200
(12) Other	40	30	15	15	100
(13) Total Direct Costs	$1,190	$ 350	$ 270	$ 290	$ 2,100
(14) Contribution to Overhead and profit (5) − (13)	$ 310	$ 650	$ 330	$ 210	$ 1,500
(15) Contribution as % of sales (14) ÷ (1)	6.2	26.0	22.0	21.0	15.0
(16) Allocated overhead	$ 500	$ 250	$ 150	$ 100	$ 1,000
(17) "Net net" (15) − (16)	(−$190)	$ 400	$ 180	$ 110	$ 500

exhorts the sales force "not to forget which side of your bread the butter is on."

• Products SS (for so-so) and AV (for average) are middle-of-the-line products. The gross profit is 40 percent of sales. Their combined volume is less than that of product BB.

• Product NP (for new product) is a promising new product being introduced in a growing market. Since it has some exclusive, patented features, it commands a 50 percent gross margin.

The first step in the analysis is to take the dollar sales income from each product (line 1) and subtract the manufacturing cost (line 3) to obtain the gross profit generated by each product (line 5). The percentages developed in lines 2 and 4 will be useful later.

Now comes the task of allocating direct costs to each product. This need not be done with hairbreadth accuracy; reasonable "guesstimates" on each allocation will serve the purpose.

Direct costs are allocated to product lines as follows:

1. *Sales costs* Calculate total costs of salaries, expenses, and investment in autos and other equipment for sales reps and managers. Include rent, staff, and other expenses of sales offices. Estimate what percentage of total selling time the sales reps spend on each product; get estimates from a cross section of sales reps and/or first-line managers. Allocate sales costs to products in proportion to the percentage of selling time spent on each.

2. *Inventory costs* This includes the value of capital tied up in inventory, insurance on it, state property taxes on it, if any, and losses from obsolescence, deterioration, or pilferage. As a very rough rule of thumb, figure inventory costs as 25 percent of the manufacturing costs of the average inventory level. Allocate these to products in proportion to dollar cost of inventory in each line.

3. *Warehousing costs* Total rental or capital investment in warehouse, maintenance, equipment, and staff. Allocate these costs to product lines in proportion to the total amount of square feet (or cubic feet, if that would be more appropriate) of warehouse space normally occupied by each product.

4. *Billing and credit costs* Calculate the total space and salary costs of the billing and bookkeeping department. Count (or estimate) the number of invoice lines devoted to each product line during a typical week or month. Allocate billing costs in proportion to the number of invoice lines devoted to each product. Credit costs include interest and collection costs on the average amount of receivables tied up in each product, plus credit losses.

5. *Shipping costs* If all products are shipped in the same way and for the same distances, simply allocate all shipping costs in proportion to the volume of products shipped in each line (or by weight, if that would be more appropriate to the type of product). If products are shipped different distances or in different ways, calculate the shipping costs incurred by

each product line—remembering that reasonably accurate estimates are sufficient, and two-decimal accuracy is unnecessary.

6. *Advertising and promotion* Allocate to each product line any specific promotional costs incurred by that line, such as advertising and direct-mail campaigns on a specific product. The balance—institutional advertising and across-the-board promotional activities—can be allocated to products in proportion to dollar sales volume.

7. *Other costs* This might include the costs of installation, customer service, instructional literature, training programs, or other activities associated with a specific product.

Direct costs are totaled (line 13) and subtracted from gross profit (line 5) to obtain the contribution made by each product line to corporate overhead and profits. Most cost accountants recommend that you stop at this point, and not try to allocate fixed overhead to product lines. It is enough to know the relative contribution made by each product to both overhead and profit.

Contribution as a percentage of sales (line 15) is obtained by dividing contribution (line 14) by sales (line 1) for each product. Note that product BB's contribution is only 6.2 percent of sales, compared with 26, 22, and 21 percent for the other three.

The reasons are quickly apparent. Gross profit is smaller to begin with. In addition, product BB, with just 50 percent of sales volume, is absorbing more than 50 percent—a disproportionate amount—of such costs as sales, warehousing, billing, credit, and shipping. .

In addition to its value in designing a sales incentive

compensation plan, this type of analysis gives management important clues on how to improve profitability of the weaker products. The out-of-line costs on product BB, for example, might be reduced by spending less sales time on it, simplifying warehousing procedures, establishing a minimum order size to reduce billing costs, and tightening up on credit policies.

All four product lines make a total contribution of $1.5 million to corporate overhead and profit. The lower right-hand figures in Table 7-1 reveal that overhead is $1 million and profit $500,000.

Why not, the reader may wonder, allocate overhead costs to each product to see what its "net net" is? Any attempt to allocate fixed overhead must be viewed with caution. What would be the logical basis for the distribution? Should overhead costs be allocated to products on the basis of dollar volume, number of units produced, gross profit, contribution, or what?

However, with the warning that the result is purely hypothetical, the last two lines of Table 7-1 show the result of allocating overhead to product lines on the basis of dollar sales volume. By these criteria, product BB is a loser, being supported by the other three.

Eliminating product BB is a last-resort measure—other cost-improvement steps suggested above should be tried first. If product BB is eliminated, the $500,000 in overhead costs arbitrarily assigned to it would have to be allocated among the remaining three products. If we again use dollar volume as the basis of this reallocation, the last two rows of Table 7-1 would look like Table 7-2.

Even if total overhead costs are reduced somewhat by the absence of product BB, it will be seen that the other three products become much less profitable when the company is deprived of BB's contribution to overhead.

TABLE 7-2   Overhead Reallocated to Remaining Three Products (in thousands)

	Product			
	SS	AV	NP	Total
Contribution to overhead and profit	$650	$330	$210	$1,190
Allocated overhead: Formerly	250	150	100	500
Share of BB's overhead	250	150	100	500
Total overhead	$500	$300	$200	$1,000
New "net net"	$150	$ 30	$ 10	$ 190

Analysis of the profitability of various types or sizes of customers can be made in exactly the same way. It will usually be found that customers below a certain size simply do not make a contribution, because direct costs exceed gross profits on goods sold to them. Such considerations of relative profitability are important in designing a sales incentive plan, especially if the objective of the plan is to increase profit dollars, not just sales dollars.

In our hypothetical case, we would want sales reps to spend less time on product BB, and more time on products SS and AV. Although the new product is already absorbing 15 percent of sales costs and contributing only 15 percent of total contribution, we might want sales reps to spend more time on it if future prospects look bright. Hence the compensation plan would give the sales rep a smaller incentive for each dollar sale of product BB and a larger incentive for each dollar sale in the other three lines.

8

ANALYZING SALES FORCE ACTIVITIES

Since one of the prime objectives of a sales compensation plan is to channel the sales rep's activities along profitable lines, the designer of the plan should know what the sales force's behavior actually is, and what it ought to be.

An up-to-date analysis of the field's activities and problems is highly desirable. Field conditions change rapidly. Many a compensation plan has failed because it was designed by a sales manager who came up from the ranks and was confident of firsthand knowledge of field conditions—forgetting that if that knowledge is three or four years old it may be obsolete.

The analyst should select a cross section of six or eight typical sales reps and spend a day or two interviewing and observing each. In many situations, the analyst should expand the cross section to cover a larger number of individuals to take into account geographical differences in field selling operations. He or she should seek answers to questions like these:

1. How much and what kind of planning should the individual sales rep do?

2. How much time does the rep spend in face-to-face selling, and how many sales calls does this add up to in the average week?

3. How are these sales calls allocated among various channels of distribution, among various types and sizes of customers, among various buying influences within a single customer company, among various products in a multiproduct line, among new prospects as compared with existing customers, among the "customers' customers" as well as the customers themselves?

4. What nonselling activities have a long-range effect upon sales productivity, how much time is currently being spent on each of them, and how much time should be spent on them?

5. How does the sales rep view his or her company's compensation plan compared with those of competitors?

6. If quotas are used in determining incentive payments, what is the attitude of the sales force toward these quotas? If the sales reps are convinced quotas are unfair or unrealistic, the motivational value of the incentive plan may be destroyed. In this case it may be better to base the incentive upon some percentage of the previous year's figures.

7. What sort of help does the sales force receive from first-line managers? Do managers receive training in how to direct the efforts of the sales force so that they will capitalize on incentive opportunities?

8. How venturesome or risk minded is the sales force? Would they like to trade part of a potential increase in their guaranteed income for the opportunity to earn several times that much in incentives?

This survey of current field practices is one area in which the outside consultant has a distinct advantage over someone from inside the company. The sales rep knows that the chances of getting a pay raise or a promotion depend upon the company management's opinion of how well he or she is handling the job, so when talking to someone on the same payroll some reps may be more interested in making a case than in presenting the facts.

In some companies the sales rep may feel it politically inexpedient to criticize some product or policy, but may be willing to express these opinions to an outsider when assured that anonymity will be preserved.

When conducting a field survey, the authors often meet the sales rep for breakfast, and the informality usually makes it easy to gain the sales rep's confidence.

"Tell me how you spend a typical day," is a good starting question, and later, "I'd just like to tag along for a while, if you don't mind."

(In making sales calls, the sales rep simply says to the customer or prospect, "This is John Jones; he's doing some work for the company, and he's with me today," and lets it go at that. If the customer is more curious, the usual explanation is that the visitor is from the home office or sales promotion department, just getting a feel for conditions in the field. If the customer or prospect is told that the visitor is a consultant, he or she is likely to spend half an hour explaining how the industry should be reorganized.)

Sometime during the day the consultant will ask the sales rep, "How well do you know the salesman from Competitive Manufacturing Company?"

"I run into him now and then."

"What do you estimate he's making per year?"

"Oh, about so-and-so."

"Would you consider swapping jobs with him?"

The answer might be anything from "I wish I could" to "They're a man-killing outfit. I wouldn't put up with all their bull; my family wouldn't stand for it."

Observation of one or two days' work is as important as the interview. Conversations with customers often reveal important functions performed by the sales rep that nobody thought to list on the job description.

THREE

DESIGNING THE PLAN

9

OVERVIEW

In designing the plan, one simply works out the answers to the questions given below, in approximately the order shown. Each topic is discussed in detail in a later chapter.

1. Which of the basic types of plans should be used?

2. What should be the total earnings of the top producer, the median producer, and the marginal salesperson or neophyte?

3. What is the split between guaranteed and incentive payments?

   a. For top producers?

   b. For median sales reps?

    c. For beginners or "tail enders"?

4. Who should participate in the plan?

    a. Salespersons only?

    b. Managers and supervisors?

    c. Merchandisers and other customer service people?

    d. Home office supporters, such as design engineers?

5. Should incentives be based upon individual performance or pooled results?

6. Will incentives be a commission on sales, or bonus for other accomplishments?

7. If some form of commission, will it be paid on all sales, or only those over a quota?

8. If a quota is used, what will it be based on?

    a. Previous sales in the territory?

    b. A company breakeven point?

    c. A target profit for the company?

    d. Estimated potential in the territory?

    e. Sales forecasts by management, sales reps, or both?

    f. Negotiation between manager and sales rep?

    g. Some combination of these?

9. What will incentive payments be based on?

   a. Sales dollars?

   b. Margins?

   c. Individual contribution to profit?

   d. Company or regional profit?

   e. Units sold?

   f. Other results of sales efforts, such as shelf space and displays?

   g. Supporting activities, such as dealer training meetings?

10. How will the plan be weighted to emphasize the more profitable products?

11. How frequently and how soon after the selling period will incentive payments be made?

12. What administrative procedures will be involved in calculating and paying the incentives?

13. How will the plan affect salary administration?

14. How can sales managers best capitalize on the plan?

15. How will it be evaluated, monitored, and if necessary, revised?

SELECTING THE BASIC TYPE OF PLAN

The designer will rarely have a free hand in deciding which of the four basic types of compensation plans to use: straight salary, straight commission, draw against commission, or salary with an incentive in the form of commissions or a bonus. Company traditions and industry habits are difficult to overthrow. Further, it is not easy to move from one basic type of plan to a completely different one. The degrees of difficulty are summarized in Table 9-1.

For the designer who does have some option in selecting a basic plan, Table 9-2 indicates which type of plan best accomplishes each of the possible objectives.

TABLE 9-1 Difficulty in Changing from One Type of Plan to Another

Present Plan	Type of plan being considered	Ease or difficulty of transition
Straight salary	Salary plus incentive	Usually fairly easy, and usually advisable
	Either type of commission plan	Virtually impossible
Salary plus incentive	Straight salary	Easy if new salaries are high enough, but why do it?
	Commission plan	Very difficult; high draw required
Straight commission	Straight salary	Unthinkable!
	Salary plus incentive	Can be done; there has been a long-range trend in this direction
Straight commission	Draw against commission	Easy; a way to provide for new hires and avoid loss of good salespersons during downturns
Draw against commission	Straight salary	Rarely advisable
	Straight commission	Difficult; draw may be needed by new people
	Salary plus incentive	Often a logical move

TABLE 9-2 Matching the Basic Plan to the Objectives

Objective	Salary plus incentive	Straight salary	Straight commission	Draw against commission
STRATEGIC				
(1) Increased volume	★		✔	✔
(2) More profitable product mix	★ (if weighted)		✔ (if weighted)	✔ (if weighted)
(3) Balance between (1) and (2)	✔ (if weighted)		✔ (if weighted)	✔ (if weighted)
TACTICAL				
(1) Motivate sales force	★ (if incentives are adequate)		✔	✔
(2) Match competitors' plans	★	★	★	★
(3) Fair to both company and sales force	★	★	★	★
(4) Reinforce desired work habits	★	★		
(5) Promote stability in sales	★	✔		
(6) Reduce or control expenses	✔		✔	✔
(7) Flexible in permitting changes	★	✔	✔	✔
(8) Aid in recruiting and retraining	✔	✔		

Objective	Salary plus incentive	Straight salary	Straight commission	Draw against commission
BEHAVIORAL CHANGES				
(1) Stress profitable products	★	★	★	★
(2) Concentrate on most profitable customers	★	★	✔	✔
(3) Promote across-the-line selling	★	✔		
(4) Control sales force; encourage nonselling functions	★	✔		
(5) Promote cooperation	★	✔		
(6) Encourage communication with headquarters	★	✔		
(7) Encourage effective sales calls	✔		✔	✔
(8) Encourage effective allocation of time	★	★		
(9) Encourage year-round sales efforts	★	✔		
.RATIONAL				
Clear, simple	★	✔	★	★
) Easy to administer	★	✔	★	★

TABLE 9-2 Matching the Basic Plan to the Objectives *(continued)*

Objective	Salary plus incentive	Straight salary	Straight commission	Draw against commission
(3) ENDS ARGUMENTS ABOUT COMPENSATION	✔		✔	✔
SALES FORCE WANTS				
(1) Adequate incentives	★		✔	✔
(2) Prompt, frequent incentive payments	★		✔	✔
(3) Balance between security and incentive	✔			
(4) Rewards individual performance	★		✔	✔
(5) Avoids unmerited fluctuations in income	★	✔		
(6) Avoids ceilings	★		✔	✔
(7) Compensation is commensurate with sales	✔		✔	✔
(8) Opportunity for promotion without financial sacrifice	✔	✔		
(9) Clear measurements	★		✔	✔

Objective	Salary plus incentive	Straight salary	Straight commission	Draw against commission
(10) No MAJOR QUOTA HARDSHIPS	★	✔	★	★
(11) No LOSS BECAUSE OF TERRITORY DIFFERENCES	★	✔		

✔ = INHERENT CHARACTERISTIC OF PLAN.

★PLAN CAN BE DESIGNED TO ACCOMPLISH THE OBJECTIVE.

10

HOW BIG IS
THE KITTY?

The subject of incentive compensation was raised during a workshop session on office management for a group of travel agency owners. One participant was shocked. "Why," she exclaimed, "that would be giving away some of your profits!"

That attitude, unfortunately, is not uncommon. Companies which view incentive payments as a sort of charitable contribution from profits are likely to be so stingy in offering such payments that they simply fail to motivate the sales reps.

As will be recalled from Chapter 4, among companies having incentive compensation plans and being dissatisfied with them, by far the biggest criticism was that the incentive payments did not motivate the sales force to work any harder or any smarter.

Incentive plans should be viewed, not as a charitable reward to the sales force, but as a profit-generating device. The basic philosophy is: "If, by extraordinary efforts, you sales reps can bring in a million dollars in profits that we wouldn't ordinarily have, we'll dish out $200,000 of it to you." Needless to say, the company doesn't disclose this type of profit analysis to the sales force, which would promptly demand that the incentives be made even greater. But the basic thought is sound: For every $1 in additional profit the incentive plan generates, somewhere between 10 and 25 cents can be redistributed to sales reps in proportion to the individual contribution of each.

Failure to offer adequate incentives is no recent phenomenon. It has existed for years, but it is worsening for several reasons:

1. As job security, fringe benefits, and pensions have been improved, additional current income has begun to seem less important.

2. The burdens and inequities of taxation have had a frustrating impact upon the middle- and upper-middle-income groups to which most sales reps and their families belong.

    a. Remedying a "bracket-creep" inequity for one rep by widening the rep's tax bracket creates a bracket-creep problem for the next higher-income rep.

    b. A Proposition 13–type cap seems to open the doors for other tax collectors to tap.

3. Inflation not only devalues the purchasing power of current dollars but also lessens the appeal of a future reward.

a. "The bonus I worked so hard for doesn't really seem like much now that I've got it," as one rep puts it.

Few of us are motivated by a shrinking carrot.

DETERMINING INCENTIVE PAYMENT TOTALS

How generous can you afford to be? A logical way to answer that question is to forecast profits for the next two or three years at various levels of sales volume. Since growth in some product lines would be much more profitable than in others, these forecasts should be made by product line. All figures should be adjusted for inflation.

Let's look at the hypothetical manufacturing company we investigated back in Chapter 7. We'll assume that sales reps allocate their time among the four product lines in proportion to the existing volume in each line. That would mean that each line would show the same percentage increase in sales. In actual life, of course, the growth rate may vary because of promotional activities, share of market, intensity of competition, and other factors which the reader can take into consideration when working with the company's actual figures.

We'll assume that manufacturing costs, as a percentage of sales, would decrease slightly because of economies of scale. We'll assume that direct costs would remain the same as a percentage of sales, and that fixed overhead would decrease slightly as a percentage of sales. (Here again the reader can make more careful adjustments in his or her own figures.)

We'll allocate fixed overhead to product lines in proportion to their dollar volume to get some idea of the "net net" available for incentive payments. (results are shown in Tables 10-1 to 10-3.)

TALBE 10-1 A 10 Percent Across-the-Board Sales Increase (in thousands)

Products	BB	SS	AV	NP	Total
(1) Sales	$5,500	$2,750	$1,650	$1,100	$11,000
(2) Manfacturing costs as % of sales, slightly reduced	69	59	59	49	
(3) Manfacturing costs	$3,795	$1,622	$ 973	$ 539	$ 6,929
(4) Gross profit	$1,705	$1,128	$ 677	$ 561	$ 4,071
(5) Direct costs, increased in proportion	$1,309	$ 385	$ 297	$ 319	$ 2,310 (21% of sales)
(6) Contribution	$ 396	$ 743	$ 380	$ 242	$ 1,761
(7) Allocation of $1,100 in overhead	$ 550	$ 275	$ 165	$ 110	$ 1,100 (10% of sales)
(8) "Net net"	$ (154)	$ 468	$ 215	$ 132	$ 661 (up 32.2%)

TABLE 10-2 A 25 Percent Across-the-Board Sales Increase (in thousands)

Products	BB	SS	AV	NP	Total
(1) Sales	$6,250	$3,125	$1,875	$1,250	$12,500
(2) Manufacturing costs, a bit lower as a %	68	58	58	48	
(3) Manufacturing costs	$4,250	$1,812	$1,087	$ 600	$ 7,749
(4) Gross profit	$2,000	$1,313	$ 788	$ 650	$ 4,751
(5) Direct costs	$1,487	$ 437	$ 337	$ 362	$ 2,623 (21% of sales)
(6) Contribution	$ 513	$ 876	$ 451	$ 288	$ 2,128
(7) Allocated overhead	$ 600	$ 300	$ 180	$ 120	$ 1,200 (9.6% of sales)
(8) "Net net"	$ (87)	$ 576	$ 271	$ 168	$ 928 (up 85.6%)

TABLE 10-3 A 50 Percent Across-the-Board Sales Increase (in thousands)

Products	BB	SS	AV	NP	Total
(1) Sales	$7,500	$3,750	$2,250	$1,500	$15,000
(2) Manufacturing costs, a bit lower still	67	57	57	47	
(3) Manufacturing costs	$5,025	$2,137	$1,282	$ 705	$ 9,149
(4) Gross profit	$2,475	$1,613	$ 968	$ 795	$ 5,851
(5) Direct costs	$1,785	$ 525	$ 405	$ 435	$ 3,150 (21% of sales)
(6) Contribution	$ 690	$1,088	$ 563	$ 360	$ 3,701
(7) Allocated overhead	$ 650	$ 325	$ 195	$ 130	$ 1,300 (8.7% of sales)
(8) "Net net"	$ 40	$ 763	$ 368	$ 230	$ 1,401 (up 180%)

The company's current profit (Table 7-1) is $500,000. Let's assume that price increases plus the company's normal growth rate would give it the 10 percent increase in sales shown in Table 10-1. Profits at this level would be $661,000.

But if the sales force can achieve a 25 percent sales increase, profits would be $928,000—an additional $267,000—while a 50 percent sales increase would produce profits of $1,401,000. This is $740,000 more than the normal growth in profits of $661,000. Could this company offer the sales force 10 to 20 percent of this—about $60,000 to $120,000—in bonuses if they succeeded in bringing it about?

If incentive payments start only after last year's figures—those in Table 7-1—have been attained, and thereafter increase from zero to $120,000 at the plus 50 percent level, sales, profits, and incentive payments would be at the levels shown in Table 10-4 and graphed in Figure 10-1.

In Tables 10-1 to 10-3, we assumed that sales of all products increased by the same percentage. Let's see what would happen if sales of product BB increased by $500,000 while those of the new product NP increased by the same amount. We'll increase direct costs in proportion to sales dollars but leave all other figures the same.

TABLE 10-4   Effect of Increases in Sales Volume

			Incentive payments		
	Sales volume	Profit	At 2.4% of sales over $10,000,000	As % of total profits	As % of profit over $500,000
Now	$10,000,000	$ 500,000	0	0	0
+10%	11,000,000	661,000	24,000	3.6	14.9
+25%	12,500,000	928,000	60,000	6.5	14.0
+50%	15,000,000	1,400,000	120,000	8.6	13.3

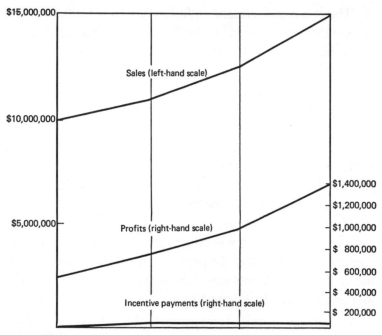

FIGURE 10-1 Effects of increased sales volume on profits and incentive payments.

Thus each additional dollar of sales in NP increases the contribution 3½ times as much as an additional dollar in product BB sales. Even if it takes the sales rep twice as long to sell the same volume in NP, it is more profitable for the company when the rep does so. Hence an incentive compensation plan for this company should be weighted in favor of NP sales.

The degree of sales effort to be expended upon a product is influenced by share of market, among other factors. Figure 10-2 illustrates graphically the relationship between market share and the results of sales efforts.

For most products, there is a practical ceiling on share of market. In a diversified and highly competitive field, for

TABLE 10-5 Comparison of Increases in Products BB and NP (in thousands)

	Product BB		Product NP	
	Now	Up $500	Now	Up $500
(1) Sales	$5,000	$ 5,500	$1,000	$ 1,500
(2) Manufacturing cost	70	70	50	50
(3) Cost	$3,500	$ 3,850	$ 500	$ 750
(4) Gross	$1,500	$ 1,650	$ 500	$ 750
(5) Direct costs	$1,190	$ 1,309 (up 10%)	$ 290	$ 435 (up 50%)
(6) Contribution	$ 310	$ 341	$ 210	$ 315
(7) Increase in contribution		$31,000		$105,000

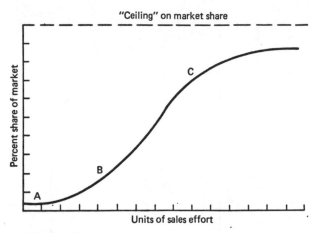

FIGURE 10-2   Stages in the development of a product.

example, it may be virtually impossible for a product to achieve more than a 10 or 15 percent share of market.

When a product is new and unknown, it takes large amounts of sales effort to win it a foothold in the market (points A to B on the curve). Then, as it gains acceptance, it becomes easier to sell and each unit of sales effort produces larger results than before (points B to C). But as the product nears the practical ceiling of its market share, it takes more and more effort to produce each percentage point of increase in share of market. The curve may eventually flatten out altogether, so that market share cannot be increased no matter how much effort is poured into the product. This relationship between sales effort and market share must be kept in mind if the incentive compensation plan is to be successful in attempting to motivate sales reps to reallocate their efforts among product lines.

Product BB, for example, may be to the right of point C on the chart. This is perhaps corroborated by the fact that it is taking up more than 50 percent of the sales effort, although producing only 50 percent of total sales. Product NP, on the other hand, is probably somewhere near point *B*, indicating that transferring a bigger share of the marketing effort to it would pay off handsomely in increased profits.

In forecasting the total amount of incentive payments, consider also the fact that different sales reps will earn different amounts. The poorer ones will earn little or no incentive money, while the real stars will earn the maximum.

If we divide a typical sales force into quartiles, and express incentive payments as a percentage of salary, the distribution of incentive payments will often look something like this:

Rank of sales rep	Lowest one-fourth	Second lowest one-fourth	Second highest one-fourth	Highest one-fourth
% of salary earned in incentive payments	0–10	10–20	20–30	30 or more

11

THE "SPLIT"

An extremely important consideration in salary-plus-incentive plans is how the proposed total income of the sales rep will be divided between guaranteed income and contingent income. What is the ideal relationship between salary (the usual form of the guaranteed portion) and the potential incentive income? What, in short, is the "split"? There is no answer appropriate for all companies or all conditions.

The guaranteed portion (salary) must suffice to provide reps with a sense of financial security; it must see them through dull seasons, as well as enable them to get started before they earn incentive money. These are only the minimal requirements. The contingent portion must of course be adequate to motivate them strongly.

The planner should first glance at what the most successful competitors do, then consider the following guidelines:

15 percent of salary extra as a minimum contingent sum.
Any less will surely not motivate.

At least 50 percent of the rep's total income should be guaranteed (salary).

This is believed to be the minimum which will enable the company to control its reps' activities.

The best range for most companies is between 25 and 50 percent of salary extra.
Certain factors will give the planner more specific guidance.

The following factors suggest a relatively high incentive element: *

- A *high degree of skill is required.* Skill may be either knowledge of the product, knowledge of its application, knowledge of the market—or commonly, all of these.

- *The company is less well known.* The sales rep working for a little-known company has, of course, a harder job.

- *The company does less advertising than its competitors.* This, too, makes the selling job more difficult.

- *The price of the product (or service) is relatively high.* This usually entails more calls, more marshaling of

*These factors were pointed out by Richard C. Smyth, *Harvard Business Review*, January–February 1968.

influential executives, and may also include proposals. All these require patience and increased selling costs.

- *There is little difference between the company's and competitor's quality.* This makes the selling job harder.

- *The career possibilities in the company are relatively low.* This makes it difficult to attract and hold good sales reps unless the potential incentive payment is substantial.

- *The selling is largely direct.* If there is no intermediary to assist with the sale, the sales rep's effectiveness is easily measured.

In the presence of these factors, the incentive increment should comprise a relatively high (say, 25 to 50 percent) proportion of the sales rep's total income.

The following factors suggest a relatively low incentive element:

- *The selling is importantly a team effort.*

- *Sales are strongly influenced by factors outside the sales rep's control.* Feast or famine products usually call for a relatively low incentive increment.

- *There is a relatively high emphasis on customer service.* The sales rep should not be tempted to neglect his or her service functions in such situations. As one respondent in our survey put it, "We don't want a hustler image."

- *The career possibilities in the company are relatively*

high. Career-oriented sales reps tends to be slightly less motivated by immediate cash incentives.

- *Advertising and promotion are strong factors in making the sale.* These tend to presell the product, making the rep's job easier.

- *The selling is largely indirect.* In situations where a wholesaler fills the order or a physician is induced to prescribe the product, effectiveness of the sales rep's efforts is difficult to measure.

In the presence of these factors, a relatively small incentive increment may be adequate, depending importantly upon the practices in the industry.

THE LEVERAGE FACTOR

Related to the question of the split between guarantee and incentive are other questions. How rapidly should incentive payments increase as performance improves? How much greater should be the incentive pay received by the star performer compared with that of the average performer?

Incentive payments can increase slowly and gradually from some base such as quota, 90 percent of quota, last year's sales, or 10 percent over last year's sales. To illustrate the point, we'll assume that the base salary is $20,000 and that the incentive payment is one-half of 1 percent of salary for every 1 percent by which sales exceed 90 percent of quota, with a ceiling of 25 percent of salary. Earnings are shown in Table 11-1 and graphed in Figure 11-1.

This type of plan tends to minimize the differences in earnings among the sales force. Note that the star performer who achieves 150 percent of quota receives total earnings that

TABLE 11-1 A Slowly Increasing Incentive Pattern

% of quota attained	Base salary	% points over 90% of quota	% of salary earned as incentive	Incentive	Total earnings
90	$20,000	0	0	$ 0	$20,000
100	20,000	10	5	1,000	21,000
110	20,000	20	10	2,000	22,000
120	20,000	30	15	3,000	23,000
130	20,000	40	20	4,000	24,000
140	20,000	50	25	5,000	25,000
150	20,000	60	25	5,000	25,000

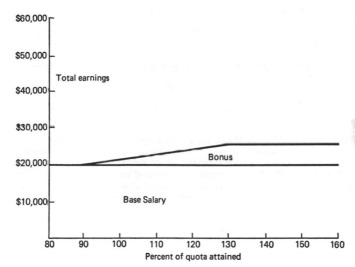

FIGURE 11-1 A slowly increasing incentive pattern.

are only $4,000, or 19 percent, greater than the income of the rep who just hits quota.

A company may decide it wants to offer relatively greater

rewards to those whose sales are significantly above the quota (or other base). There are three possible reasons for this:

1. To provide additional motivation that will prevent sales reps from slacking off in their efforts when they exceed quota by 15 or 20 percent

2. To boost company profits when the marginal increment of profit on additional sales volume is high

3. To retain the star performers by offering them big earnings

One way to accomplish this might be to pay 1 percent of salary for each 1 percent of sales over quota, up to 50 percent of salary. The results are shown in Table 11-2 and graphed in Figure 11-2.

Under this program, the rep who is 50 percent over quota has earnings that are $10,000, or 50 percent, greater than the rep who just makes quota. This upward leverage in incentive

TABLE 11-2 A More Rapidly Increasing Incentive Pattern

% of quota attained	Base salary	% points over quota	% of salary earned as incentive	Incentive	Total earnings
90	$20,000	0	0	$ 0	$20,000
100	20,000	0	0	0	20,000
110	20,000	10	10	2,000	22,000
120	20,000	20	20	4,000	24,000
130	20,000	30	30	6,000	26,000
140	20,000	40	40	8,000	28,000
150	20,000	50	50	10,000	30,000

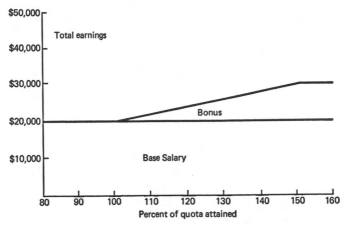

FIGURE 11-2 A more rapidly increasing incentive pattern.

payments can be heightened by increasing the percentages of salary received for higher over-quota achievements. For example, the plan might offer:

- ½% of salary for each 1% of quota from 90 to 110%

- 1% of salary for each 1% of quota from 110 to 130%

- 2% of salary for each 1% of quota over 130% (with or without a ceiling)

Results of this plan are tabulated in Table 11-3 and graphed in Figure 11-3.

In this pattern the person who achieves 50 percent over quota has earnings that are $13,000, or 61.9 percent, greater than those of the person who just hits quota.

So, in addition to considering the average split between guarantee and incentive, the plan designer must also determine how much leverage to build into the plan. In most cases it is

TABLE 11-3 A Highly "Leveraged" Increasing Incentive Pattern

% of quota attained	Base salary	% points over 90% of quota	% of salary earned as incentive	Incentive	Total earnings
90	$20,000	0	0	$ 0	$20,000
100	20,000	10	5	1,000	21,000
110	20,000	20	10	2,000	22,000
120	20,000	30	20	4,000	24,000
130	20,000	40	30	6,000	26,000
140	20,000	50	50	10,000	30,000
150	20,000	60	70	14,000	34,000

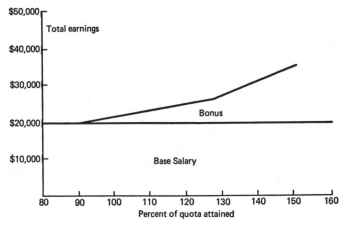

FIGURE 11-3 A highly leveraged incentive plan.

considered important to establish a marked difference between the earnings of the outstanding sales reps and the run-of-the-mill performers.

12

WHO PARTICIPATES, AND TO WHAT EXTENT?

There are three problems involved in deciding who should and who should not receive incentive compensation: (1) the problem of identifying who made the sale, (2) the problem of splitting incentive credit or commissions when one or more individuals has participated in the sale, and (3) the related problem of team incentives versus individual incentives.

Some businesses have none of these problems; others have all of them, and resolving them is seldom easy.

IDENTIFYING THE SELLER

A typical problem arises at the retail level: A prospective customer enters the establishment and asks to look at, shall we say, widgets. The salesperson makes an effective presentation, pointing out the quality features of the widgets, their reasonable price, and their superior styling. The prospect is impressed, but wants to consult his wife; after all, this widget is a fairly high-ticket one.

The next day, the prospect returns with his wife, but the salesperson he saw the day before is off that day, so another salesperson takes over, and gratefully closes a potentially difficult sale with surprising speed.

Which salesperson made the sale, the first one or the second?

A similar situation often arises in the direct sale of an item of capital goods to a prospective user. The prospective customer has had several interesting discussions about the capital goods item with Sales Rep A. The next year, when Sales Rep A has been transferred to another territory, Sales Rep B calls upon the prospect, who decides that this is the right time to buy. So Sales Rep B gets an easy order.

Perhaps a two-salesperson presentation may be made; after all, Sales Rep Jones knows more about double-barreled widgets than Sales Rep Brown, whose territory it is. At the suggestion of their field sales manager, Jones accompanies Brown on a call and the previously reluctant buyer signs an order.

Still another type of problem in identifying the seller frequently occurs when the sale is made for the distributor to deliver and invoice. This situation presents serious complications when—as often happens—the distributor is either unable or unwilling to set up accounting procedures so the manufacturer can identify which of the sales reps got the order.

A frequently encountered example of divided responsibility occurs when the buying office at the national headquarters of a corporation must authorize all purchases made by branches or regional offices. The sales rep calling on the tough buyer at headquarters makes a difficult sale when the buyer agrees to put the product on the approved list. But purchases are made only when the local sales reps persuade local buyers to order. Who gets how much of the credit for each sale?

SPLITTING INCENTIVE CREDIT OR COMMISSIONS

It is easy to see how any of the previously described situations can suggest the possibility of splitting incentive credits or commissions. Even more frequent, at least in certain industries, is the situation where there are multiple buying influences, one or more of which may be located in the territory of a different salesperson.

A solution that has worked moderately satisfactorily in engineered product lines when this situation is present is to allocate, say, 25 percent sales credit to the rep who worked with the prospect's engineers and developed the specifications, 50 percent to the rep who worked with the contractors and got the order from the successful bidder, and 25 percent for the rep in the territory who serviced the installation. Other splits are also used, such as a four-way split, when the product is purchased through a distributor.

In the award of major contracts, these credit and/or commission splits can be very important to the salesperson or persons entitled to them. In some cases, custom-tailored splits may be in order.

> One manufacturer's sales rep worked for many months to get a substantial order for new instrumentation to be installed in all models of a certain type military aircraft—present ones as well as all those to be built in the future. Installation on present models was to be done at one designated airfield, with the work scheduled over a period of months.
>
> Two sales reps shared the sales credit. The major share, more than 75 percent, went to the individual who got the original covering contract, and some 25 percent to the individual

serving the installing airfield. (The latter performed mainly a paperwork processing function.)

Another example of a customer-tailored split was established by a manufacturer whose materials were being used in major quantities in the Alaskan oilfields.

The specifying engineers were located in New York City, the customer was in Philadelphia, a supervising engineer was in Houston, the material was shipped by a Seattle distributor, and finally installed in Alaskan oil fields.

It was important in this situation that the salespersons responsible for each location be strongly motivated to carry through the local phase of the work, and that top-notch communications be maintained all along the line. Admittedly, this chain of influences was unusually long, but the volume of materials being specified, ordered and installed was substantial. Salespersons at five locations were "in the act," and it was imperative that all of them be dealt with equitably.

Pharmaceutical company sales executives have become so frustrated over trying to determine "who created this prescription" that many of them have abandoned efforts to offer sales incentives based on individual achievement.

PAYING FOR INDIRECT PARTICIPATION

Questions frequently arise regarding the payment of incentive compensation to individuals who participate indirectly and/or infrequently in the selling process. Such individuals have contended with considerable logic that the chief sales correspondent, certain technical product or service specialists, and the like should be awarded incentive bonus credits and/or commissions in recognition of work they do which has undeniably influenced sales decisions.

In the authors' judgment, awards for such services should never be made part of the sales incentive compensation plan. Once incentives are paid *as a regular feature of the sales incentive plan* to individuals whose regular duties are not face-to-face contact with customers and prospective customers, it becomes exceedingly difficult to decide where to stop. If incentives are paid for indirect, nonselling activities, there is serious risk of demoralizing the field sales force and vitiating the value of the incentive plan as a motivating force.

Bonuses are occasionally awarded with beneficial results to home office executives participating in the closing of a major contract award, or even to technical product specialists who contribute importantly to a big sale, *but such awards have almost never been a regular feature of the regular sales incentive plan.* They may be awarded frequently, but out of a special discretionary executive bonus fund.

In summary, the authors strongly favor limiting participation in sales incentive compensation to those individuals whose regular duties involve face-to-face contact with customers and prospective customers. Sales supervisors, although part of the field sales force, do not ordinarily spend most of their time face-to-face with customers, and therefore should have a separate incentive compensation plan of their own. More about this later.

Service personnel, city order desk clerks, and others are often in frequent contact with customers and logically say that they influence sales. But the question is "If you bring them into a compensation plan, where can you stop?"

In one compensation study on which the authors worked, the city sales manager, who handled incoming telephone orders, made the point: "The salesmen see a customer only once every two weeks, but I talk to them twice a day. Why can't I be in on these sales incentives?"

We went to the VP sales and asked him, "If we let the city desk folks into the plan, where do we stop?" His answer: "Don't start."

In technical fields of selling, questions often asked are: "Aren't the design engineers and the installation engineers just as important to the company as the sales force?" "Don't they make an equal contribution to company profits?" "Then how can it be fair to offer incentives to the sales force and not to these backup people?"

It is not a question of relative importance—everybody is important to the company. Discussions about relative importance are like asking which is the most important leg on a three-legged stool. The real question is, "Is the nature of the work such that a variable income will produce better results than a fixed income?" As mentioned earlier, the salesperson is subjected to so many frustrations, disappointments, and generally demotivating circumstances—much more so than the inside people—that it seems reasonable to offer an extra incentive to maintain motivation.

GROUP INCENTIVES VERSUS INDIVIDUAL INCENTIVES

Where a choice is possible, an individually based incentive plan is nearly always preferable to a group-based plan.

Group plans tend to be more successful where there are exceptional communications between and among those individuals making up the group. Good communications permit one member of the group to assist and/or encourage another, or to constructively needle the other members of the group when desirable.

Group plans tend to be less successful where communications among the various members of the group are difficult or nearly nonexistent because of distance or other factors.

> Two sales reps, each in a far-flung territory, generate all or nearly all of a certain manufacturer's business with a distributor located about midway between their two sales territories. The best measure of each sales rep's performance is the distributor's sales, but the distributor either cannot or will not supply a breakdown between the two territories. The two salespersons rarely have a chance to meet or communicate because of distance.
>
> The group-based incentive applying to these two salespersons is regarded by all parties as something less than wholly successful.

Many times in situations of this kind a way can be found to combine an individually based plan with the group plan.

> For example, a large grocery manufacturer has split distribution; i.e., while most of the sales are made through distributors, some important accounts are sold direct.
>
> The rank-and-file sales reps are eligible for a group-based plan based on distributor sales, but the standout sales reps, considered candidates for early promotion, may also service one or more of the direct-buying accounts on an individual incentive basis. This affords them higher income opportunity than those on the group plan. It also gives their performance better visibility to management.

Another example of how group and individually based plans have been successfully combined is shown on a product (rather than on a customer) basis.

In a certain company, the product line is wide and technically complex. Each sales rep knows the major products in the line thoroughly and also knows some of the minor products as well, but no one sales rep can be considered thoroughly expert in *all* products. Since the sales reps work out of regional offices, their opportunities to get help from or give assistance to their colleagues are good.

Accordingly, major products are eligible for individual sales incentives (based on individual quotas), while the minor products are eligible for a group bonus (i.e., pro rata bonuses if the office makes its team quota).

Another way to combine group and individual bonuses is to alter the sequence in which each bonus is made available. For example, all individual bonuses earned might be increased by a given amount or percentage if the group (team) meets its quota.

One company which responded to the authors' survey pays an incentive which is based 70 percent upon individual sales, and 30 percent upon the profitability of the district. The sales manager reports that the plan stimulates both individual efforts and team cooperation.

There are many ways an ingenious plan designer can combine group and individual bonuses to offset the weaknesses inherent in most group plans.

INCENTIVE PLAN PARTICIPATION

At one time there was a school of thought which held that, in order to motivate the sales force, it was not necessary for all eligible members to participate. This viewpoint has fortunately fallen by the wayside. The present view is that all eligible individuals should have an opportunity to earn incentive—if not an *equal* opportunity, at least an *equitable* opportunity.

Equitability of participation can, of course, never be assured by management. One step management can take to improve equitability is to make incentive opportunities available *only to those individuals with at least a minimum of seniority.*

Above and beyond such a step, however, management's only obligation in regard to participation is to make the never-ending effort to assure each salesperson a territory of more or less equal potential, and to set reasonable quotas if quotas are involved.

One of the signals of future trouble is a decreasing participation in the sales incentive plan with fewer and fewer sales reps earning incentive. Decreasing participation is, however, not always the fault of the sales compenstion plan or its administration.

In general, the company where two-thirds or more of the eligible sales reps earn some incentive is probably following a sound course and management is doing a good job of sales incentive administration.

13

WHAT AND WHAT NOT TO PAY FOR

Every marketing executive knows his or her marketing objectives, and a quantitative sales goal is sure to be one of the most important of these. Problems can arise, however, whenever the executive undertakes to incorporate into a compensation plan specific incentives intended to do any of the following:

1. Control in detail the products to be stressed, and how many or how much of each

2. Include a reward for carrying out specified nonselling duties, at least some of which could not have been anticipated in advance

3. Pay a higher incentive for new accounts than for sales to established customers, for sales of new

products, for sales made at full markup instead of at an authorized lower or fallback price, and similar practices

In short, incorporating multiple objectives in a sales incentive plan has to be undertaken with caution, lest the designer vitiate the effectiveness of the plan. As a general rule, the greater the number of sales objectives the designer includes (in excess of two or three), the weaker the plan.

The more numerous the objectives management offers to pay for,

1. The less reward money is available for each objective

2. The more ingenuity is required in designing the plan *and*

3. The higher and more attractive the incentive features and indeed the whole compensation package should be

Basically there are three types of objectives:

1. Quantitative sales objectives: These can be in terms of dollars, tons, or units and can be weighted as to profitability.

2. Quantified nonselling objectives: Install X number of displays, conduct Y number of distributor sales meetings, or arrange for shelf space.

3. Unquantified or judgmental nonselling objectives: Maintain good customer relations, report market information, show initiative, and be loyal to the company.

Quantified sales objectives are easy to measure and are readily understood by the sales force. Complications arise when the incentive payment is based on some quota of dollars or units.

A quota accomplishes two things:

1. It keeps sales costs lower when volume is below target.

2. It motivates the sales force to strive for volume. If a rep doesn't achieve quota (or come close to it), there is no incentive payment at all; above quota, each sale contributes to incentive payments.

Because a sales rep can be financially penalized by an unreasonable quota, the quota-setting process merits careful consideration.

SETTING QUOTAS

Whether quotas be expressed in units, dollars, or gross margins, their establishment is one of the most demanding jobs the chief sales executive is called upon to perform.

Quotas can be derived from several sources.

Sales Reps' Forecasts   Many companies ask each salesperson to forecast the next year's sales, by product lines, for the territory. These figures are usually negotiated upward or downward by the manager in conferences with individual sales reps.

Studies have shown that there is no built-in bias in forecasts made by the sales force. Some individuals tend to be optimistic, some tend toward more conservative estimates, but in total their estimates are reasonably accurate.

Some companies keep a record of each rep's forecasts and

results over a period of years and thereby develop a correction factor to be applied to future forecasts, based on the individual's historic tendency to overestimate or underestimate future sales.

Even if sales reps' estimates carry little weight in quotas eventually established, they are worth collecting because they give the sales force some feeling of participation in company planning, and require them to do some thinking about the size of the potential market for the various products in their territories.

Corporate Marketing Goals In some companies, top management sets the companywide goals for each product line. These goals are then divided among regions and districts roughly in proportion to their previous share of company sales. Each first-line manager then takes the target handed to him or her and divides it among the individual sales reps in accordance with the abilities and opportunities of each.

Sales Potential Figures A company which has developed accurate measurements of geographic sales potential can use these figures in setting quotas.

A carpet manufacturing company sets quotas this way:

1. In territories where sales are below potential, the quota is half the distance from present sales to 100 percent of potential. For example, an undeveloped territory producing only 50 percent of its geographic potential would be given a quota of 75 percent of potential.

2. For other territories, the quota would be a standard percentage increase.

Sales reps tend to distrust potential figures. This is partly because of the "decimal-point delusion." When a sales rep is told his or her territory should produce 0.001873 of national sales, the rep knows nobody can measure the potential in that territory with four-digit accuracy.

The best way to handle this is for management to say, "Our calculations show that potential sales in your territory are 0.001873 percent of national sales, which amounts to $187,300. But we realize measurements of potential aren't all that accurate—all that we can be sure of is that potential sales in your territory are somewhere between $175,000 and $200,000, so we're setting your quota at $175,000."

Previous Sales An easy but not too accurate method of setting quotas is simply to expect each territory to produce the same percentage increase over the previous year's sales. The trouble with this method is that it's much easier to get a given percentage increase in an undeveloped territory than in one in which sales are nearing saturation.

Salespersons for an industrial distributor came up with an ingenious means for basing quotas on past sales volume. They pointed out to the boss that if contests were based on increases in dollar volume, the well-developed territories would be favored; if they were based on percentage increases, the underdeveloped territories would be favored.

Suppose one territory is producing $1,000,000 in sales and another territory $250,000. If the company bases contests (or quotas) on an increase in dollar volume, the first territory has a cinch. An increase of $50,000 represents only 5 percent more sales, while the same dollar increase in the second territory is a 20 percent increase. On the other hand, quotas based on a percentage increase favor the smaller territory. It can achieve a 10 percent increase with just $25,000 in additional sales, whereas the larger territory must boost its sales $100,000 to show a 10 percent increase.

The solution devised by the sales force: Base quotas or contest points on the *square root* of previous sales. The square root of $250,000 is $500, of $1,000,000 is $1,000. If the quota is set at 10 square root units over last year's figures, the larger territory would get a quota of $1,010,000 (an increase of $10,000), the smaller one a quota of $255,000 (an increase of $5,000). The sales reps felt this represented equal difficulty for the two territories.

Sales Forecasts   Sometimes a company can find leading indicators that forecast its sales trends rather accurately. For example, a firm making construction materials may find that the ups and downs of its sales parallel the ups and downs of construction permits or new housing starts after a delay of some months. Where such forecasts are available, they are useful in setting quotas.

Breakeven Points or Profit Targets   A company may set sales quotas at the point where the company breaks even, or attains a profit goal; the idea is that profits above this point are shared with the sales force.

For example, a welding supply distributor in New Jersey determines the volume at which his company will break even. On all sales above that figure, each sales rep gets 1 percent and the sales manager 3 percent. This is, in effect, a pooled bonus based on a breakeven quota.

Production Capacity   In some situations, a company may find it necessary to consider its production capacity when setting overall sales objectives, then make tentative allocations of such capacity.

CALCULATING INCENTIVES BASED ON A QUOTA

In some companies the incentive is an all-or-nothing proposition based on the achievement of quota. If a rep's sales don't exceed quota, no incentive is earned. This plan makes the quota itself unnecessarily critical. If the quota is even a bit too high, the sales rep is not motivated, he is discouraged. This difficulty can be somewhat alleviated by starting incentive payments when sales reach, say, 85 or 90 percent of quota. True, the amount of the incentive will still be reduced if the quota is too high, but it is reduced rather than eliminated.

A manufacturer of industrial equipment uses a simple plan which keeps incentive payments within reach of all sales reps. Incentive payments start when sales reach 85 percent of quota; the rate is 0.7 percent of salary for each percentage point over the 85 percent base. Maximum incentive is 20 percent of salary. Typical incentive payments are:

% of quota achieved	% points above the 85% base	% of salary paid as bonus (column 2 x 0.7)	Bonus amount for sales rep earning $18,000
85	0	0	0
90	5	3.5	630
95	10	7.0	1,260
100	15	10.5	1,890
110	25	17.5	3,150
120	35	20.0	3,600

Note that this plan, which has been used for many years, relates bonuses to salary levels. This maintains the desired split between guaranteed and contingent income, because higher salaries automatically produce higher potential bonuses.

Another difficulty with quotas is the effect of inflationary price increases. If a company raises its prices 7 percent in the course of a year, every sales rep who would otherwise have just hit quota is automatically selling at a rate 7 percent above quota.

There is little objection to this during periods of moderate cyclical inflation—say, up to about 5 percent yearly—because the designer of the plan has usually factored that much of a price increase into his quotas, or doesn't mind paying a relatively modest incentive earned by achieving 5 percent over quota.

The effects of inflation can be somewhat reduced by using the "target area" or "steplike" method of increasing incentive payments. As illustrated in Figure 13-1, the commission or incentive rate is the same at anywhere from 85 to 105 percent of quota. For a sales rep near the middle of such a bracket, an increase in dollar volume resulting from a price increase will not result in a higher incentive level.

QUOTAS SHOULD NOT ALWAYS BE SACROSANCT

Too many companies regard the quotas they have established as sacrosanct. "The controller has them entered against us," their sales executives say. However, the sanctity of quotas vitiates their potential value in possibly cutting a loss.

The authors recall a situation where a sales rep, through no fault of his own, suffered the loss of his major distributor early in the quota period. The rep, whose record had been good but heretofore undistinguished, made a herculean effort, and managed to replace the loss (with two new distributors) late in the quota period. Customers were once more getting served, and everything was moving satisfactorily; however, the quota

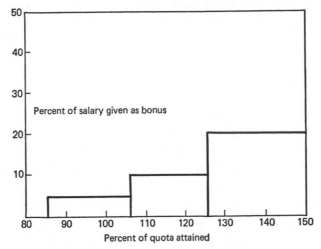

FIGURE 13-1 A steplike pattern of incentive earnings.

performance results for the period were a disaster. To reward the sales rep, management gave him the largest salary raise his bracket would allow. But no bonus—"He didn't earn any."

The sequel: The sales rep could not get another increase for a considerable period, and eventually left the company. An excellent plugger type, he was not easily replaced. How much better it would have been had the company immediately given him a better-than-normal salary increase, cut his quota, and permitted him to earn a good bonus.

Such situations—frequently multiplied when there is a recession—are not uncommon. Some flexibility in quotas can be very advantageous under such conditions.

OTHER QUANTIFIED SALES OBJECTIVES

Still another approach successfully used by a growing number of companies is to establish quotas in terms of *physical units* such as tons or truckloads or cases.

In a complicated product line, one major product may serve as the product unit, with other products representing varying numbers of these product units. In one widely known plan, for example, sales of office equipment are measured in typewriter units, with a standard typewriter representing one unit, a fancier model being counted as two or three units, a copying machine as perhaps six or eight units, and so on.

Developing and achieving agreement on physical units, if a different weighting is to be assigned to some of them, requires considerable planning and thorough indoctrination of all members of the sales organization—especially, of course, the field sales force. It entails a major communications effort. For this reason many companies, especially those with heterogeneous product lines, still use dollar sales objectives.

Another type of quantitative sales objective is the setting of a gross profit or net profit quota. Setting a net profit quota is usually too complex an accounting job to be acceptable, but the gross profit target is attractive, especially to wholesalers; most reps selling at wholesale know their gross margins, and computerized accounting can calculate incentive earnings with reasonable speed.

A word should be said in behalf of multiple quotas—quotas for each product line or product group, not just for total sales. These quota plans, if made interesting to the salespersons and if imaginatively and aggressively administered, can be quite successful. They are uniquely appropriate where sales reps sell the products of several distinct product groups to the same trade channels, each of which may (or may not) be a profit center.

A publishing company had five different product lines—say, for example, fiction, textbooks, children's books, playing cards, and board games. The common denominators were that they were all produced mainly on a printing press and sold in discount department stores.

To encourage full-line selling, management gave the sales rep a quota on each product line, based on past sales in the territory. The sales rep received an incentive payment at the minimum rate if he or she made the total gross sales total, plus the individual product quotas on any two of the five product lines.

If the sales rep reached total quota plus the quotas on three individual product lines, the bonus rate was larger. The maximum bonus rate was paid to the sales rep who hit total quota plus all five product line quotas. There was no problem motivating the sales force to do a balanced selling job while this plan was in effect and was well administered.

A division of Diamond-Shamrock Company sold a group of laundry and dry-cleaning products which varied greatly in profitability. The same principle was followed: There were four product groups differentiated not by type of product, but by profitability. Maximum bonus was earned by the sales rep who achieved quota on all four product groups, lesser bonuses by sales reps who achieved total quota and two or three of the product group quotas.

This particular plan got the benefit of some unscheduled and unusually imaginative administration, in that one of the junior sales executives, at the end of the first two months in each quarter, would telephone each of the 20 to 30 sales reps to point out how much bigger the next quarterly bonus would be if the rep got to work on whichever product group was lagging. In addition, memos went to each sales rep before the end of the quarter projecting his or her bonus for the quarter (Figure 13-2). There was space—not shown in this illustration—in which the sales rep could insert a higher target figure and quickly calculate how much more of which products he or she needed to sell during the last month of the quarter to earn the higher bonus.

	A	B Laundry	B Drycing	C	D
2nd QUARTER INCENTIVE CALCULATOR					
Incentive Groups					
A. Quarter-to-date sales		9,250.00	0	17,943.00	6,578.25
B. Quarter-to-date quota	N/A	4,561.74	219.39	13,191.75	1,656.24
C. Quarter-to-date sales over quota: A-B		4,688.26	N/A	4,751.25	4,922.01
D. Multiply result by commission rate	%	4%	%	1%	1%
E. Commissions earned		187.53		47.51	49.22
Total commissions earned	284.26				
Bonus, if earned: 20% or 10%	28.42				
Total earnings	312.68				
Salesman: R. Smith					
Calculator:					

Incentive calculator. Salesmen can use this form to determine the bonuses they have earned—or how much more they must sell in a given quarter in order to earn a bonus.

FIGURE 13-2 This memo, sent to sales reps before the end of the quarter, indicated how much incentive they had earned so far, and enabled them to calculate what their sales had to be for the last month in the quarter to achieve any earnings goals they wished to set for themselves.

At the end of a year the profit contribution of this division of Diamond-Shamrock had increased by 29 percent—a fantastic improvement.*

There is occasional use of a *composite* numerical quota combining such factors as unit sales, dollar sales, price maintenance, and sales expenses. While these composite quotas

---

*For a more detailed description of this incentive plan and the training program that accompanied it, see "Revitalizing a Sluggish Sales Force," *Business Management* magazine, 1966.

provide some incentive for the sales force to keep within expense budgets and resist off-price selling, they are frequently not meaningful to the sales force and in some cases have been misused by the plan administrator. The greater the number of elements factored into the complex quotas, the greater the likelihood of confusion, resentment, and resulting turnover of personnel.

Most companies have not had much long-term success with sales incentive plans which undertake to emphasize new accounts or full-price business. Emphasis on new accounts is, in most situations, better achieved by means of short-term or medium-term special drives or contests, while the problem of making cut-price business less attractive for incentive purposes may be better handled by combining sales goals with gross margin goals.

This can be done either by using a composite quota, as discussed, or by using multiple quotas—one for sales, the other for gross margin, with substantially higher awards for the rep making both quotas.

NONSELLING OBJECTIVES

Salespersons are often called upon to carry out many nonselling tasks such as collecting overdue bills, advising on the extension of credit, building displays, forecasting inventory requirements, servicing the customer's equipment, and the like.

Most companies requiring considerable nonselling duties of this type make some time allowance for the salesperson expected to perform them, or may even specify approximately how many displays must be set up and similar tasks. The sales quota may be adjusted slightly downward to compensate for time lost on these duties. Sales incentive plans rarely provide any specific award for carrying out such duties.

It is sometimes possible to quantify nonselling objectives. One example is the building of displays by salespersons calling on retail stores.

A company selling grocery products required its sales reps to build 10 displays of a specified minimum size each month, as evidenced by snapshots taken by the sales rep with a camera provided by the company. No matter what else was accomplished, the sales rep did not recieve a bonus unless he or she had achieved this display objective.

JUDGMENTAL OBJECTIVES

Judgment-based awards of various kinds enjoyed some popularity a couple of decades ago, but are currently little used. The main reason is that poor administration has led to perfunctory judgments, judgments inconsistent from one supervisor to another, and a tendency to award judgment incentives on "soft" criteria, particularly during periods of inflation.

For example, one type of criterion was the accomplishment of company-required market research. Another involved the training of a neophyte salesperson. Both of these duties tended to slow down the sales rep assigned them, and therefore some recompense in the incentive plan was deemed advisable.

In our experience such judgmentally based criteria are usually ineffective and inadvisable. Too often this type of objective involves subjective factors, such as the quality of the sales rep's presentation, or whether or not the presentation covered all the selling points specified in the official sales manual. Awarding bonuses based on such criteria is likely to become a misused practice, and is best avoided.

In the one successful plan based partially on judgmental criteria, which the authors installed in recent years, the sales force was small and compact, communications had always been

excellent, and the administration and operation of the entire plan was, from the start, closely monitored by top executives. This plan has been quite successful, but the conditions essential to its success were uniquely favorable.

MIXING QUANTITATIVE AND JUDGMENTAL CRITERIA

Our reservations about mixing quantitative and judgmental conditions are the same as those applying to nonquantitative objectives generally: the quality of the judgments can so rarely be assuredly sound and consistent that we have rarely used them. Furthermore, in the inflationary climate of the past several years, the best way to reward judgmentally evaluated performance is probably with a salary increase. Certainly the salary increase will motivate better, and with the tendency to make salary increases considerably less uniform from one sales rep to another, it is believed that this route will be more widely followed in the future than "one shot" judgmental bonuses.

One rule to be observed whatever method is utilized is to set quotas and objectives: The more participation in the goal setting management can get from its sales reps, the more effective its incentive plan will probably be. Reps like having a voice in establishing their goals, even if the quotas they suggest are "negotiated" upward. Parenthetically it should be noted that where sales reps are consulted, they frequently set higher objectives for themselves than those management wants to establish.

14

HOW AND HOW MUCH TO PAY:
Commission Plans

Although commission-only plans, with or without a draw, are used by less than 30 percent of the companies responding to our survey, it is logical to discuss this type of plan first because many of the considerations involving straight commissions also apply to commissions which are part of a salary-plus-incentive plan.

SCALED COMMISSIONS

With a commission-only plan, some companies pay relatively high commissions on the first big portion of sales volume to enable beginners to make a living, then smaller commissions on additional volume to prevent runaway sales costs.

A company in the soft goods field paid a commission of 12 percent on the first $100,000 of sales. Since this company's sales job offered potentialities for rather explosive earnings, sales over $100,000 were commissionable at declining rates, according to this table:

Sales volume	Commission rate, %
Up to $100,000	12
$100,001 to $300,000	7
$300,001 to $500,000	5
Over $500,001	2

All sales reps provided their own cars and paid their own expenses.

Ascending and descending commission scales are rather common in some industries. If the initial commission rates are generous, it is not difficult for a trainee sales rep to achieve a satisfactory income rather quickly. Thus the company has no problem in attracting good sales personnel. On the upside, total annual earnings in excess of $50,000 (before expenses) are easily possible, given historical territorial volumes.

PROBLEMS OF SCALED COMMISSIONS

When the initial commission rate is high, the decreasing rates at greater volumes strongly suggest the need for an unlimited or "unceilinged" total compensation. Yet this lack of a ceiling can bring serious problems:

1. Jealousy from sales personnel in less strongly established territories. As B. K. Moffitt, a compensation plan consultant, expresses it, "A sales force with several lovable veterans who are being paid twice as much as equally productive men of lesser seniority is likely to be a sales force with a low morale."

2. Loss of management's ability to control the amount and quality of sales effort in the territory.

3. Envy on the part of knowledgeable home office personnel, possibly leading to poor cooperation and service.

Moreover, a scaling of commissions tempts sales reps to manipulate their inflow of orders.

In the previously cited case, it was not difficult for a sales rep who had booked substantial December volume to hold back some of it until January, thus assuring that the business would be commissionable at the 12 percent rate instead of at a 5 or 2 percent rate. There are no easy answers to either of these two problems.

In the first case, where unceilinged total earnings may be costing a company its control over a territory, if that territory is a major market either actually or potentially, it might be better to change its compensation plan. The decision would surely be a difficult one.

In the second instance, where scaling incentives (whether in the form of commission or bonus) is seriously disrupting order flow and production planning, as well as frustrating the aims of the compensation plan, there are several possible options:

1. Management may take a hard-nosed attitude, deciding which commission rate or fiscal period to accept, and refusing to discuss its decisions afterward.

2. Management may rule that only in-house orders and/or orders accepted by the production department will count, with regard to the fiscal period and the

incentive rate. (This would almost certainly increase the communications costs of the more distant reps.)

3. Management may design an incentive scale in which there is a smooth transition from one incentive pay level to another, without any discrete jumps. Instead of the steplike method illustrated in Figure 13-1, the incentive payments can increase gradually as shown in Figure 14-1.

In one company, the sales force used this type of chart and a ruler to check on their level of incentive payment. Since there was only a slight increase in the incentive percentage from one performance level to the next, there was less incentive to manipulate order flow.

The planner can set the commission percentage and quota performance requirements wherever his or her company wishes, or cost/profit projections indicate. With the same commission

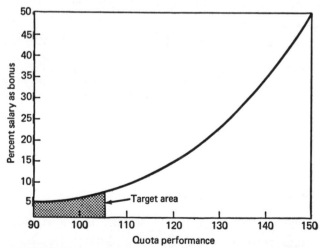

FIGURE 14-1 A gradual transition from one incentive level to the next, minimizing the temptation to manipulate orders.

rate at anywhere from 85 to 105 percent of quota, there is little incentive for a rep to manipulate order flow within that area. The commission rate "tops out" by running off the chart—a form of ceiling.

RETROACTIVE COMMISSIONS

Some companies have used retroactive commissions as special medium-term motivational devices. Here is an example:

> Upon being assigned a new, difficult, but high-potential account, the sales rep was given the following incentive package in regard to this account:
>
> 1. The regular bonus schedule, which could pay up to 15 percent of salary (with, of course, a low estimate for the new account included).
>
> 2. A retroactive extra commission at a small rate on *all* sales that had been made to the new account during the past year (including all those before it was assigned to the rep) provided there was a carload order from the new customer before the end of the year. It was estimated that this would probably amount to about $2,000 extra for the rep.

COMMISSION ON GROSS PROFITS

This type of incentive, long used by many wholesale organizations, is being used increasingly by other types of organizations which sell a variety of lines (or services) carrying differing gross profit margins.

Sales personnel in wholesaling, and many in retailing (in contrast with those of manufacturers), nearly always know the gross profit margins on the products they sell. As a consequence, a commonly used incentive plan for wholesalers is a salary plus a percentage of the gross profits, or markup. The now nearly universal availability of computer services has made this type of incentive increasingly attractive for the manufacturers. It is uniquely appropriate for the company which sells a diversified product line, yet produces only certain products itself.

EQUALIZING OPPORTUNITY

In any type of commission plan, all sales personnel should have equitable earnings opportunities. If there are assigned territories or accounts, territory boundaries should be drawn or accounts assigned in such a way that potential sales in all territories are as nearly equal as possible. Geographical sales potentials can be calculated from industry sources, or from buying power surveys like those published by *Sales and Marketing Management* magazine. In an undeveloped territory, higher commission rates are sometimes paid to compensate for the extra time and effort that must be devoted to missionary selling.

For retail sales personnel on commissions, the opportunity to work during prime selling time must be equitably distributed among all salespersons. This is seldom a simple task: comparing commissions earned with hours worked is only a beginning. The sales executive has to take into account such factors as:

- Availability of the various sales personnel for work during prime selling hours of the week
- The income needs of the various sales personnel
- Their respective skills and talents
- The attitude of the union, if there is one

DRAWING ACCOUNTS

Some of the devices used in conjunction with commission plans are old; others are relatively new. Among the former are *drawing accounts* and salaries. Less common (until comparatively recently) are commissions based on gross profit margins on the goods or services sold. Such plans have been facilitated by computer calculations.

Drawing accounts are almost as old a device as commission itself; they are, in essence, simply advances against future commission earnings. In the past, drawing accounts were adhered to more or less strictly; the sales rep not earning his or her draw was terminated, or, as old-time managers expressed it, "They eliminated themselves."

Today, drawing accounts tend to be adhered to somewhat less strictly; as the saying goes, "It's front page news when a company collects a drawing account overdraft." Today's manager of draw-versus-commission sales personnel virtually walks a tightrope between writing off an overdraft and taking the risk that the overdrawn salesperson will either get into the black or quit and make a fresh start somewhere else. In such cases, the draw becomes in effect a salary. Many companies write off their overdrafts yearly. When such situations are frequent, there is sometimes a strong temptation for the company to go to a salary-plus-commission plan.

Table 14-1 shows how those who responded to our questionnaire treat the problem of overdrafts on drawing accounts. The sample is small, since relatively few respondents used a draw-against-commission plan, and many of those failed to answer this question. The available replies, however, indicate the variety of solutions to the overdraft problem.

TABLE 14-1 How Companies Handle Overdrafts on Drawing Accounts (Figures are actual numbers of respondents mentioning each method)

Deduct the following percentages of the overdraft from the next commission check:	
100%	10
50%	2
25%	1
Carry the overdraft forward for the following period of time, after which it is settled or the salesperson is terminated:	
Indefinitely	3
Next pay period	1
30 days	2
60 days	1
One quarter	3
6 months	1
1 year	2
4–5 years	1
Reduce or discontinue draw until overdraft is made up	6
Write off overdrafts (practically a small-salary-plus-commission plan)	6
No overdraft occurs, usually because draw is relatively small	5
Establish a ceiling on the amount of overdraft	1
Varies with individual case	1
Pray!	1

15

HOW AND HOW MUCH TO PAY:
Salary-Plus-Incentive Plans

In this type of plan there is a guaranteed salary plus an incentive payment based on individual or group performance. The incentive may be:

1. A *commission*, the term used for a payment based on some percentage of sales or gross profit dollars

2. A *bonus*, meaning the payment of a fixed dollar amount or a percentage of base salary for superior results as measured by quotas, the previous year's sales, or specified marketing objectives

3. A combination of commissions and bonus

DEFINING TOTAL EARNINGS

The first step in planning a salary-plus-incentive program is to establish the total income range for each category of sales personnel. The figures might look something like this:

	Minimum	Median	Maximum
Sales reps	$15,000	$20,000	$25,000
National accounts reps	$20,000	$25,000	$30,000

These figures are usually based on the present earnings of the sales force (adjusted for inflation), competitors' plans, industry surveys, turnover rates, and a liberal sprinkling of horse sense. The total income figures are usually set at levels which approximate the income levels established by competitors. A survey of competitors' pay levels provides the necessary information.

As intimated earlier, competitive compensation levels are not the complete and final answer. If competitors are long-established and have a history of giving their sales forces excellent training and advancement opportunities, their sales reps may be compensated slightly below the market. A slight premium over going levels may, in such a situation, attract and hold high-caliber sales reps.

Consideration must also be given to the width and probable profitability of competitors' product lines. It is not always necessary to meet competitors' pay standards dollar for dollar. Generally, however, it is wise to offer at least as good *total* earnings opportunities.

HOW TO PAY

The decision of how to pay the projected sales incomes is not so clear-cut. Many companies have deliberately held down sales reps' salary growth slightly for a year or so, in order to be able to offer meaningful incentive opportunities later. They do this because an incentive not adequate to motivate may, in most cases, be regarded as wasted effort, maybe even wasted money.

WHAT KIND OF INCENTIVE—COMMISSION OR BONUS?

A commission is usually a specified percentage of sales, whereas a bonus is usually a designated sum awarded for specific achievements. The most important difference between the two is that a commission is frequently open-ended, whereas a bonus is ordinarily not. Where there is no objection to an open-ended award, and where management wishes to avoid any appearance of a "cap" or ceiling on sales reps' earnings, the commission incentive is commonly used.

Commission incentives can make high-earning sales reps unavailable later for promotion to management level positions. Where such considerations are not a factor, there is little objection to using commission incentives, other than the fact that they frequently make it difficult to properly control the sales force or reward team selling.

The bonus is, by definition, a finite, more-or-less readily determinable amount. Whereas runaway incomes caused by windfall sales are usually possible with a commission incentive, this is rarely true with a bonus incentive plan. Either method can provide good motivation, according to how the plan is designed.

Since many sales reps are ambitious and consider themselves upwardly mobile, they may prefer a bonus-type incentive—one which, assuming that the company is growing and has good salary administration, enables them to aspire to managerial level promotions. The fact that a bonus plan is, in effect, a sort of cap on their total earnings is not too objectiona-ble, provided the ceiling is not too obvious and bonus oppor-tunities are reasonably generous.

In the final analysis, the decision between bonus and commission incentive is likely to be a corporate one, made for the incentive plan designer rather than by him or her.

Company traditions, industry customs, whether or not explosive commissions are likely, whether—if they should occur—they would prove disruptive, and whether management considers its sales force a reservoir of talent for future executive positions—all these will influence the decision.

ESTABLISHING THE BASE SALARY

Setting salaries with a salary-plus-incentive plan is perhaps the most difficult step. The halfway house idea of paying a small salary and liberal commissions is increasingly unpopular; if a salary is paid, it is usually a substantial one.

In changing to a salary-plus-incentive plan from either a straight salary plan or some form of commission plan, the planner's initial analysis should include a study of the total earnings of each sales rep for at least a few years. Reference should also be made to the total earnings of competitors' field sales personnel. Management and the planner must decide on the split (or "incentive reach," as some personnel executives call it).

Formal job evaluation and position rating are frequently dispensed with, unless other factors such as personnel turnover, territorial splits, or inflation make them necessary.

Sales reps' salaries do not fit neatly into the standard job evaluation procedures companies commonly use for inside positions. The typical internal employee usually works as a member of a group, under continuous supervision. The outside sales rep works mostly alone, with infrequent direct supervision. The rep who has built up a profitable territory is often reluctant to accept any mathematical formula as to what his or her salary should be.

Because of this, sales reps' salary brackets and salary increases have often been largely based on judgment. For similar reasons, many companies establish wider salary brackets for their sales force, create more than one category of sales position, such as junior, senior, national accounts, or combine both of these techniques.

The salary should be adequate to free the salesperson from worries about ordinary living expenses. It should be adequate to "get by on" during a downturn in the economy and in sales volume.

A salary is considered by today's sales rep as an indication of his or her worth to the company. It is a form of recognition. A sales rep who has consistently shown good quota performance is unlikely to be motivated without some degree of recognition in the form of salary increases, even though total earnings may be more than adequate.

One of the advantages companies cite in support of their salary-plus-incentive plans is that, normally, it is not necessary to raise the salaries of sales reps eligible for incentive compensation as rapidly as they do for other salaried employees. In view of the pace of inflation during the latter 1970s, everybody, bonus candidate or not, has been getting COLAs (cost-of-living adjustments) or salary increases by whatever name. Most companies still make a conscientious effort, however, to distinguish between merit increases and cost-of-living increases, usually by making the former larger than the latter (if deserved).

Also, companies increasingly stress the need for balance in

their salary-plus-incentive plans, recognizing that, when increasing sales reps' incomes, they must consider three elements: merit increase of salaries (if deserved), cost-of-living increase in salaries (when required), and increasing the incentive opportunity so it will still continue in proper relation to the salary.

The survey asked this question:

> Do you consider—between the further inflation many people expect and the administration's proposed wage-price guidelines—that you may want to revise your sales compensation upward during the coming year?

Of those replying "Yes" or "Probably" (41.2 percent of those answering this question), a plurality (43.7 percent) expected to increase both salary and incentive payments, compared with 28.1 percent who planned to increase salaries only and 36.2 percent who planned to raise incentives.

> One manufacturer with a salary and incentive plan gives a bonus based 30 percent on budget performance, 20 percent on work habits, 25 percent on initiative (specifics include new customers, specification work, market and account penetration) and 25 percent on judgment (with specifics including problem solving, job knowledge, accuracy, and similar skills)—all as rated by the rep's superiors on a quarterly basis. The manufacturer thus can keep in regular touch with the quality of the sales rep's progress (salary factors) in addition to having the usual data on the rep's quota standing.

THE BONUS FORMULA

A bonus can be expressed in a variety of ways, as either a designated sum of money or a formula readily convertible to money, such as a percentage of salary.

There is one point strongly in favor of the percentage-of-salary approach, and that is that it establishes a fixed relationship between the bonus and the salary maintained throughout the plan: the split between guaranteed income and contingent income, once decided upon, is preserved throughout. And, as we have seen, the split is important.

There are no limitations upon the plan designer, however; he or she can utilize percentage points, and give each point a value or proceed in the desired way so long as the result is clear.

ARITHMETICAL CONSIDERATIONS

The incentive plan designer will find it an asset to be skilled in mental arithmetic, and to have a calculator at hand. Not all potential arithmetical boobytraps are obvious, and testing as you go is prudent. The designer may, for instance, encounter a situation where a small base (quota or subquota) is dangerous to work with, and other situations where a large base also presents hazards.

In dealing with multiple quotas for sales territories, for instance, situations like the following may arise:

Total quota for period	Total new product (NP) group quota for period	Total regular product (RP) quota for period
100	20	80

Total quota may be based on long experience, but new product group quota may easily be wildly optimistic or overly pessimistic; it is often the result of hope, a market test made somewhere else, or guesswork done without detailed knowledge of the customers and prospects in the territory. The rep may double his NP subquota, or attain none of it.

Paying on a percentage increase, or paying an open-ended commission for sales over quota, is a high-risk approach. The safer procedure would be to bracket the performance criteria widely, offering, say, an adequate reward for 80 to 120 percent of the NP quota, a good reward for 121 to 200 percent, and an excellent but not open-ended reward for performance over 201 percent of the NP quota, and reserving more precise criteria until some experience has been gained.

Similarly, a large base can be risky.

> In one regional manager's plan, the vice president, relying on recent figures and the "inertia of large numbers," offered his managers $500 for each percentage point by which their performance exceeded 95 percent of their difficult-looking quotas.

> Performances and bonuses were in the normally expected range save one, where the regional manager went 40 percent over quota because of a sales surge resulting from a local weather disaster. The $20,000 bonus left a happy manager incredulous over his luck, four other managers envious, and the vice president red-faced.

In other companies, sales and profit performance have also been volatile beyond recent experience. The analyst should be especially wary when working with open-ended commissions and percentage increases.

Another, more subtle arithmetical hazard is in establishing bonus or commission scales on an inconsistent basis—not ascending rapidly enough to motivate, or ascending so rapidly that manipulation of the inflow of orders is encouraged.

Ideally, the planner should try to avoid an overt, stated-outright ceiling, but if a relatively high one is used, it will probably not lessen motivation significantly. The planner can also utilize commissions in combination with bonus devices, provided he or she keeps in mind the open-ended nature of such commissions.

Many companies use a scaled bonus plan, in which incentive is calculated as a percentage of base salary but this percentage is scaled either upward or downward as sales volume increases. Bonuses scaled downward seem to be used mainly at the upper end of bonus awards. The decreasing bonus percentage serves almost as a ceiling on earnings. Bonuses scaled upward are more common.

One manufacturing company offers its sales reps this scaled bonus plan:

Sales performance	% salary as bonus
Under 70% of quota	No bonus
70 to 80% of quota	$100 flat bonus
80 to 90% of quota	0.4% of salary for each percentage point above 80%
90 to 110 of quota	1.0% of salary for each percentage point above 90%

These awards are additive. For example, a rep at 101 percent of quota received the $100 flat bonus, 4% of salary for the 10 points between 80 and 90 of quota, and 11 percent of salary for the quota points between 90 and 101 percent.

Salaries, fringe benefits, and expense accounts are maintained at competitive levels in this company, but there is a bonus ceiling of 40 percent of salary. Because the company sells industrial products, and very large sales are not uncommon, the ceiling has generated almost no negative reactions. With occasional minor changes, this plan has been used successfully for many years.

Several respondents to the survey conducted in connection with this book used scaled commission or bonus plans. One of them noted that the ease of forecasting sales was an important advantage.

One difficulty with scaled bonus or commission plans is that they may tempt sales reps to manipulate the timing of orders. If the incentive is scaled downward, the rep may defer year-end orders to the following year, when they will command the higher initial rate. If the incentive is scaled upward, reps will be tempted to load customers at year-end because orders are in the higher incentive bracket. One way to reduce this tendency is to increase or decrease the incentive in steplike increments, as described on page 118.

COMMISSIONS AS INCENTIVES

A commission based on sales volume is, of course, the most widely used incentive device and the most easily understood. When used as part of a salary-plus-incentive plan it can create for management the risk of paying excessive amounts.

Companies facing the danger of runaway commission earnings use various devices to put a ceiling on earnings, such as:

1. Establishing a cap on the amount of commissions which will be paid in addition to the salary

2. Having the commission apply to only a limited volume of sales

3. Limiting the amount of windfall commission that may be earned on any one order, or from any one customer

4. Reducing the commission rate above a certain volume level, to the point where motivation is lessened

5. Reducing the size of territories

Unless the company is willing to set a liberal upper limit (as one company responding to our survey does, capping commissions at 100 percent of salary, or making the commission rate apply to sales of a relatively determinable sales volume which is not open-ended), management may want to consider some of these devices. This is unnecessary, of course, if the potential sales are not volatile.

16

WHEN TO PAY

Two basic questions concerning the timing of incentive payments are: "How often should incentives be paid?" and, "If delivery or payment is made long after the sale is made, how soon should the incentive be paid?"

FREQUENCY

Every sales rep likes to receive any earned incentive promptly after earning it. Speedy payment makes for better motivation. For the analyst in doubt about frequency of payments, a quick survey of field force wishes plus administrative feasibility is suggested. Unfortunately, this precept is often disregarded.

Incentive plans calling for payment of a year-end bonus are especially criticized by sales reps on this score. The behavior of a sales rep in January is very little influenced by some vaguely defined lump-sum payment to be received 14 or 15 months in the future. Most companies using such plans could substantially improve the motivation of their field sales personnel by paying more frequently.

Long-delayed incentive payments are sometimes effective where salaries are generous and the sales force almost without exception tends to earmark bonus money for special purposes such as reducing a mortgage, making investments, or providing for a child's education. Generally, however, sales reps who use their income in such planned ways are in the minority. This leads to a general principle:

> Payment of incentives earned should in most cases be made as frequently as possible without making the sums so small that they do not seem worthwhile.

The reason is that more frequent payments tend to become part of the sales rep's spending habits and thus motivate throughout the entire quota period. Given the prevailing computerized payroll accounting, this extra motivation is usually well worth the trifling cost.

The authors frequently recommend (or find) a quarterly payout system.

> One manufacturer of gift items reported that he paid bonuses annually, but that they were highly effective in motivating the sales force. The explanation: Sales reps received a *monthly* statement of how much they had earned during the previous month and year to date. This served as month-to-month motivation, while the annual payment was a much more substantial sum of money than one-twelfth of it would have been.

TIMING ON DELAYED DELIVERIES

Many manufacturing companies cannot sell their finished product out of inventory, or even give prompt delivery. They must wait until a custom-designed product has been produced.

Service industries often have a similar problem: the service is rendered and paid for long after the initial contract is signed. Sales executives for such companies face a choice that is frequently difficult: whether to pay incentive compensation when the order is booked, when it has been delivered or invoiced, or when it has been paid for.

Company policies established by top management usually establish the parameters for such decisions.

Several factors are considered:

1. What has been the cancellation experience with regard to the company's customers? What is industry practice?

2. How long a period of time normally elapses between booking and delivery? How long is the procurement and manufacturing cycle?

3. At what point during this cycle does the company have to make its biggest investment?

4. In event of cancellation, approximately how much of this investment is salvageable at full cost value, at less than full cost value, or is scarcely salvageable at all?

5. What is the total value (at cost) of the product sold?

6. What, if any, are the responsibilities of the sales rep during the design and manufacturing processes?

Two or three basic types of incentive plan payments are found in companies that face these problems:

A manufacturer of heavy custom-built equipment, sold to industries where cancellation is virtually unknown and where the salesperson has some liaison work to do during the design and manufacturing stages, pays incentive compensation upon bookings.

Another custom-built equipment manufacturer selling mainly to governmental units, and in an industry where cancellation is virtually unknown, pays incentive upon delivery.

A manufacturer of custom-designed equipment for offices pays a split incentive: part on booking, part on delivery.

This last situation presents the most difficult problem of all, namely, how much of the total incentive to pay at each stage.

Computer sales personnel generally get about half (or less) of their total incentive at booking, and the remainder after installation. At one time some manufacturers in these fields paid a relatively heavy "front-end load," and the remainder at installation. Recently, the even split has been more common, and there is currently a trend toward an even heavier "back-end load."

The planner is seldom asked to plow virgin soil; generally the customs of the industry and the responsibilities that attend each phase of the selling job dictate what course to take.

The designer must walk a tightrope between how to motivate the sales rep and how to carry out *all* phases of the job, bearing in mind on the one hand that a long-deferred award (heavy back-end incentive and long manufacturing cycle) may not motivate strongly enough to secure the orders, while on the other hand a big front-end load may lessen the interest in carrying out responsibilities after the order is booked. Progress payments on account during the manufacturing process, and the problem of whether the product will be sold or leased, can further complicate the problem. Most manufacturers who have tried various timing programs find the 50-50 or 40-60 split the most satisfactory.

In nearly all such situations, total incentive is and should be a large portion of the salesperson's total income. In a typical case, incentive is likely to reach 75 percent or more of base salary.

17

EXPENSES AND FRINGES

Policies regarding traveling expenses and fringe benefits are usually determined by industry customs or company traditions (sometimes by union negotiations!), but common practices can be summarized.

SALES REPS' EXPENSES

Although it is common for sales reps on a commission basis to pay their own expenses, the more widely-used procedure is for the company to give the sales reps a budget (usually negotiated after a study has been made) to cover travel, living, and entertainment expenses (T&E, in the vernacular). Extra rewards for holding expenses below budgeted levels or penalties for exceeding budgeted levels were abandoned by most companies long ago. Actually, the sales rep who consistently spends more than the sums budgeted is probably either producing superior results, or should be terminated. The feeling is that the sales rep (unless he or she is a problem operator) should not be demotivated by pettifogging negatives which save little money.

Automobile Expenses

Surveys are constantly being made of the practices connected with sales representatives' automobiles. Other than a general trend toward use of smaller cars and the urging of reps to utilize the telephone more, fuel shortages have apparently had little effect on practices in this area.

Most companies supplying their sales reps with automobiles have rules against personal use of such cars (not always enforced). There are undoubtedly compensation aspects associated with personal use of company cars, or allowances paid to sales reps for using their own cars. Such allowances may be worth up to $3,000 a year. For the present, this remains a substantial fringe benefit to a sales job.

Relocation Expenses

Although relocation expenses are not part of a compensation plan, it is good procedure for a company to have a stated policy. Transferring a sales rep from one location to another is done much less frequently than it was a few years ago. There is one good, solid reason: Many of today's reps, and more specifically their families, will not accept frequent transfers. Another reason is the ever-increasing cost the transferring company is expected to assume. There will always be exceptions, however, and some individuals still welcome an occasional transfer.

In a recent survey by the authors, the following practices were noted:

Item	Comment
(1) Moving household effects	(1) Invariably paid for by the transferring company
(2) Cost of at least one or two trips to the new location for employee and spouse, including varying amounts of "expensable" motel and board while house hunting or awaiting possession	(2) Invariably paid for by the transferring company
(3) A more-or-less fixed sum for miscellaneous expenses such as new draperies	(3) Invariably paid for by the transferring company
(4) Real estate commissions and settlement costs	(4) Commonly paid for by transferring company
(5) A cash bonus of $500 to the spouse to compensate for the inconvenience	(5) Sometimes paid for by the transferring company

These payments have become almost the rule in relocating a sales rep with any seniority.

Extremely few companies actually guarantee a transferee against loss in the exchange of houses. However, in the booming real estate market of recent years few losses have been incurred. The transferee usually receives a substantial salary increase, making a small loss on real estate a relatively unimportant factor in the decision.

OTHER FRINGE BENEFITS

Table 17-1 indicates, for each type of compensation plan, the percentage of users providing various fringe benefits. The figures are percentages of those answering this question, a total of 399.

TABLE 17-1 Fringe Benefits

	Benefits in percentages provided by those using:				
	Salary plus incentive	Straight salary	Straight commission	Draw vs. commission	All
Medical plans:					
Fully paid by company	62.9	46.3	16.3	29.6	55.4
Partly paid by company	27.9	32.8	22.4	32.1	32.3
Total	90.8	79.1	38.7	61.7	87.7
Life insurance:					
Fully paid by company	63.3	55.2	24.5	32.1	58.6
Partly paid by company	25.5	22.4	12.2	14.8	24.3
Total	88.8	77.6	36.7	46.9	82.9
Pension plan:					
Fully paid by company	48.2	49.3	12.2	24.7	45.1
Partly paid by company	11.6	9.0	4.1	2.5	9.8
Total	59.8	58.3	16.3	27.2	54.9
Profit-sharing plan:					
Fully paid by company	33.5	32.9	12.2	22.2	32.6
Contributory savings plan 75	5.2	6.0	0	2.5	4.8
Total	38.7	38.9	12.2	24.7	37.4
Vacations:					
Fully paid by company	90.4	86.6	20.4	14.8	76.9
Partly paid by company	2.8	7.5	2.0	6.2	4.5
Total	93.2	94.1	22.4	21.0	81.4

Fringe benefits correlated more closely with the type of compensation plan than with the nature of the industry: manufacturing, distribution, or service.

Paid vacations are almost universal among companies with either type of salary plan, but are paid to only about one-fifth of salespersons on a commission basis.

There has been an increasing tendency to provide some fringe benefits to commission salespersons. Note that more than one-third of sales forces on a straight commission basis receive fully or partly paid medical plans and life insurance, and about half of those on a draw-against-commission receive these benefits. Sales reps, even those in the sometimes dog-eat-dog life of a straight commission, are gaining recognition as "people."

CONTESTS, MERCHANDISE AWARDS, AND TRAVEL

The authors have no bias against travel and merchandise awards for sales reps, provided the companies using them do not regard them as substitutes for money.

Travel and merchandise awards seem to have been most productive where:

1. They are available to third parties who play an important role in the selling, i.e., distributors' sales personnel.

2. They are not used frequently.

3. They are used innovatively, with some element of surprise, or as a feature of a short-term campaign or contest.

4. Their usage has some background in industry custom.

Where any of these conditions are present, travel and merchandise awards can be very useful. It is not necessary that all the conditions listed above be met. Sales contests, when they are used, have proven most effective when limited to a period of about six weeks. Similarly, merchandise and travel offerings work best if restricted to a comparatively short period. The awards made available should be in addition to the money available through the sales rep's regular incentive compensation plan.

18

WHAT ABOUT ADMINISTRATION?

In designing any compensation plan, one must give realistic, hard-nosed consideration to the important problem of how the proposed plan will be administered and, more specifically, by whom. Time and again both internal designers and external consultants have refrained from submitting sophisticated and relatively complicated plans because of doubts about the company's ability to administer them. All too frequently, basically good plans have been misused or discarded because the administrator who made them work left the company or was promoted, and the successor was neither as efficient nor as dedicated.

The analyst must make a realistic judgment while designing the plan: If a good administrator isn't available, a simpler and possibly less desirable plan should be considered. The designer must not overtax the capabilities of those who will probably administer the plan.

It is an excellent idea for the designer to consult with the probable administrator of the plan before it is completed and submitted to the planner's superiors. It will be helpful if the prospective administrator not only knows the details of the plan, but understands the thinking behind its various features.

The authors' experience plus their conversations with employers contacted during the field survey undertaken in connection with this book all indicate that the administration of sales incentive plans is one of the places where the potential for improved profitability is overlooked to the point of neglect.

The experience of Diamond-Shamrock in imaginatively and aggressively administering the sales incentive plan installed in its Textile Care Division leads us to believe that the results achieved by them—in improved sales and profitability—were at least 10 percent better than might have been obtained had they merely followed the more perfunctory accounting-oriented administrative procedures ordinarily followed by most companies.

The ideal solution—for companies that can justify it—may well be to have this administrative function performed by a member of the controller's staff having line responsibility to the marketing manager. Such a relationship can frequently assist in ways other than administering incentives.

The mechanics of adminstering sales incentive plans are usually simple. The emphasis should be on the following:

PROMPTNESS

A promptly paid incentive motivates better than a delayed one of equal size.

MULTIPLE QUOTA PLANS

Such plans must receive careful and meticulous administration. Reference is again made to plans such as those used by

Diamond-Shamrock and the publishing company cited in Chapter 13.

SALARY POLICIES UNDER SALES INCENTIVE PLANS

These can become a trap for the unwary, especially under inflationary conditions. Too often, they lead to one of two serious deficiencies:

1. Sales salaries are increased at the same rate as cost-of-living adjustments are for other salaried personnel, without an increase in incentive. The salary can reach a level where the amount of the bonus offered no longer suffices to motivate the sales reps.

2. Salary adjustments for field sales personnel are neglected when COLA is made, on the premise that their incentive compensation payments will suffice to keep their total incomes abreast of the increased cost-of-living. This situation—if allowed to continue—can cause undesirable turnover, especially when bonuses shrink because of depressed sales volume.

It cannot be emphasized too strongly that when inflation dictates an increase in the incomes of field sales personnel, both the salary element and the incentive should be increased. Otherwise, incentives can shrink to the point of nonmotivation, and salaries may rise to the point where it is difficult to offer the sales personnel further potential for career advancement. These considerations are especially important for the company which considers its field sales personnel a reservoir of executive talent for future needs. They serve to document the wisdom of maintaining wider-than-ordinary salary brackets for field sales personnel.

Under conditions of 4 or 5 percent yearly inflation (such as prevailed a few years ago), it was not always necessary to give field sales personnel eligible for incentives a salary increase every year. This is one of the advantages of a good incentive plan.

19
DRAFTING
THE PLAN

Drawing up the plan is basically a matter of cut-and-fit—develop a tentative plan, run it through the testing process described below, refine it, and test it again. This is especially true if the designer can try his or her ideas on the chief marketing executive and the top financial officer at certain points during the work. Cutting, fitting, testing, changing, and then repeating the process can be laborious, but facility in finding shortcuts comes with experience.

Analysts drawing up an incentive plan for the first time might well consider imitating a plan they and their fellow executives admire, inserting their own company's figures, and then meticulously determining what modifications need be made.

In drafting a plan from scratch, designers will find the

sequence of questions given in Table 19-1 useful, as well as the list of alternative approaches given in Table 19-2.

A few hints on selecting or designing incentive formulas:

1. A scaled formula, with incentives starting at, say, 90 percent of quota and increasing in percentage, makes for accceptance by the sales reps. They are even more aware than is management of the difficulty in setting quotas.

2. Although most sales reps say they would prefer an unlimited incentive (no cap), they will usually accept an upper limit on their incomes if equitably established, generous, and not made an obvious feature of the plan. One way of doing this without seeming too obvious is to offer the same maximum dollar bonus for all sales above, say, 150 percent of quota. The formula should be designed in such a way that in any given fiscal period very few of the field sales person-

---

TABLE 19-1 Basic Questions in Plan Design

(1) What should the median total income be?

(2) Of this amount, how much should be represented by salary—i.e., what's the split?

(3) What should the range of salaries be?

(4) How should the range, and the individual salaries, be established?

(5) How will incentives be calculated? (See Table 19-2 on alternative methods.)

(6) How will quotas be set?

(7) When and how often will incentives be paid?

TABLE 19-2 Alternatives Available

ON THE BASIC PLAN

Straight commission

Commission against draw

Straight salary

Salary plus bonus

Salary plus commission

COMMISSION OR BONUS CALCULATIONS

On sales-over-quota or from dollar no. one

On sales dollars or gross profit

Across-the-board, or varying by product line

Fixed or scaled; if scaled, either upward or downward with increasing volume

Pooled or individual

Ceiling or no ceiling

INCENTIVE CALCULATIONS

Commissions of any type listed above

Attainment of other quantified objectives

Attainment of judgmental objectives

TIMING

Frequency of payment,
proportion of incentive paid at
booking, delivery, payment of invoice, or progress payments

nel will actually have their total income curtailed by the cap.

3. The formula should also be drawn so that, with the possible exception of first-year sales reps, at least two-

thirds (and preferably more) of all sales reps should earn some incentive.

4. Caution should be used in combining percentage gains with specific dollar awards, since in many businesses rather wide percentage gains (or losses) are not unusual. This is especially true with new products, and with new or small territories.

One company offered its field sales personnel a $500 bonus for each percentage point by which sales were over quota. This figure was based on several years of past history which showed customary performance ranging from 5 to 8 percent over quota. One individual who was given a relatively low quota exceeded it by some 40 percent, qualifying for a $20,000 bonus—far more than had ever before been paid. This had a demoralizing effect on the rest of the sales force.

TESTING THE PLAN

It is a serious error to defer the testing of a preliminary plan until the last step. Such deferral can produce a difficult corner to back out of, and can cause more preventable wasted effort than almost anything else in the field of incentive compensation plan design.

The analyst's mind should be fixed on the recent income statistics of the group he or she is undertaking to compensate; the total earnings and split of the median salesperson, and the analagous data for the high and low individuals.

Once a tentative formula has been worked out and tentatively agreed upon, it is time to test the plan in terms of the effect on the company's profits and on the individual sales reps of:

1. A good year

2. A poor year

3. A new product introduction or, conversely, a product withdrawal

4. A change in territories

5. A windfall sale

6. A runaway sales volume in a higher-commission line

It's also an excellent idea to calculate total direct selling costs, as a percentage of gross sales, for a good, poor, and median year. Top management will usually want these figures. And always, of course, the analyst should be asking how each tentative plan satisfies the objectives established earlier. Table 6-1 will be useful here.

Where the number of field personnel is relatively large— say, 100 or more—it may be satisfactory to test the proposed plan against a random sample of the actual individuals covered. For example, a recent plan for a 110-person sales force was tested against some 30 field sales engineers, 10 district managers, and 25 service technicians. Less numerous categories were fully tested.

Until the analyst gains experience in the design of incentive compensation plans, it's a good idea to subject any tentative formula to this type of testing *before* trying it on for size with the marketing vice president and the controller.

FOUR

SELLING THE PLAN

20
INTRODUCING
THE PLAN

Since any tinkering with a compensation plan impinges upon the sales rep's pocketbook nerve and triggers highly emotional reactions, a new plan or a major change in an existing one must be very carefully introduced. The important points are to make sure the plan is clearly presented and well understood, and to assure sales reps that they will have the opportunity to earn more money, but at the worst will not earn less money.

If the plan can be introduced to the entire sales force at a national sales meeting, a good outline to follow is:

1. Explain the plan very carefully, using good visuals and giving the sales reps a printed copy to follow.

2. Have each sales rep calculate what the next year's earnings will be with various volume levels, product mixes, or other components in the plan.

171

3. Allow plenty of time for questions.

4. Give each sales rep his or her quota figures, and allow time for individual sessions with the manager to discuss the plan and the quotas.

If there is no opportunity to present the plan to all sales reps at a national meeting, a good substitute procedure is to make video tapes of top executives explaining the plan, and then to show these tapes at regional meetings. These days, every company has access to a nearby video taping studio, and every regional office can rent a tape deck and monitor for viewing the tape.

One company had 150 sales reps in the field, and needed to present the plan quickly to the entire sales force. The consultants prepared an audio tape explaining the plan. The VP sales and two of his assistants used this as a guide in making their own tape, with the VP sales doing the explaining and the two assistants asking the questions that would likely come up in the field.

These three top executives then went out into the field, each covering four of the twelve sales regions. At these regional meetings, attended by the first-line district managers, the headquarters executive first explained the plan live, then gave district managers copies of the tape to take out to their districts. The DM's added their own comments to the second side of the tape and sent these tapes to their salespersons. At the next district meetings, sales reps were given their quotas, plus an opportunity to ask any questions.

If the compensation plan is to be explained to the sales force by mail, it is the authors' practice to draft a letter to go out over the chief sales executive's signature. The letter explains the highlights of the plan, and the details are covered in an enclosed memo. The manager's letter usually ends with, "Good selling, and I hope you make a lot of money out of the opportunities presented by this new compensation plan."

A company can make its incentive compensation plan more effective by frequently promoting the entire plan, special features of it, or new provisions of it. This can be done by means of letters to sales reps from the sales manager, flash bulletins, or news items in personalized bulletins received by the sales force. If, for example, the company is currently seeking additional distribution, a bulletin to the sales force can show how incentive earnings will be increased as a result of sales volume obtained from new dealers or distributors.

The success of incentive plans in general, or of particular features of an incentive plan, is not always assured by a mere accounting-type announcement of the plan's provisions. The plan must be continually merchandised to the sales force—especially in these days when heavy front-end deductions emasculate the motivational benefits of the incentives offered.

Helping Sales Reps Capitalize on the Plan

The existence of an incentive payment plan does not automatically bestow upon sales reps the skills they need for developing the maximum profitability from their territories. Time and territory management is a complicated subject which few sales reps acquire by instinct. Sales management must provide policies and guidelines to help sales reps capitalize on their incentive opportunities, and to insure that the company receives maximum benefits from the plan. This chapter will outline some of these procedures.

Those sales executives satisfied that their sales reps already plan their sales coverage with optimal efficiency, and then systematically carry out these plans, may want to skip many of the portions which follow.

Those who feel their reps could do better, and especially those having reps who are not too experienced, will find this material useful if only in getting their reps to devise systematic and efficient coverage programs of their own.

Given the emphasis devoted to incentive compensation plans that enhance profitability, some discussion of more efficient time and territory management seems appropriate.

OBJECTIVES

The first step in territory management is for the sales rep, at the beginning of the calendar, fiscal, or selling season year, to set down the specific objectives for the territory.

These would include:

- Total sales, by product or by product line

- Total sales by customer types or categories

- Total sales, and specific marketing plans, for a handful of critically important key accounts

- Any objectives pertaining to the rep's type of selling, such as new customers, dealers, or distributors acquired, maximum accounts receivable levels or credit losses, expense levels, and items of a similar nature

SALES CALL ALLOCATION

The most difficult task facing the sales rep is to determine how to allocate the limited number of sales calls among the various types and sizes of customers.

Too much time spent with small customers means that the potential of the larger accounts is not adequately developed. Too much time spent with the big accounts means that smaller but growing customers may be neglected. Too much time spent with existing accounts means that not enough new accounts will be opened.

How can the sales rep determine the optimum call frequency on each customer and prospect?

Figure 20-1 shows the projected annual sales volume expected from *one* customer with varying frequency of calls.

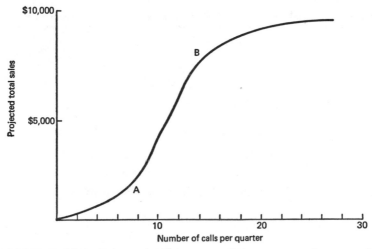

FIGURE 20-1 Relationship between call frequency and projected sales.

If the sales rep makes too few calls, he or she fails to develop a share of the potential business. At five calls per quarter, the chart indicates, the rep would expect only $1,000 in orders.

At the area of the curve between points A and B, additional calls produce enough additional volume to justify the call. Ten calls per quarter can be expected to produce $5,000 in volume from this hypothetical account, and fifteen calls should bring in $8,500.

After point B the curve flattens out. The sales rep has passed the point of diminishing returns; additional calls do not produce enough additional volume to justify them. The expected sales results from 20 calls per quarter are $9,500—only $1,000 more than the total produced by 15 calls.

If we divide the expected sales volume by the number of calls required to produce it, we get the significant figure for average sales per call. In this case the averages would be:

Number of calls	Expected sales	Average per call
5	$1,000	$200
10	5,000	500
15	8,500	567
20	9,500	475
25	9,750	390

These results are plotted in Figure 20-2.

With this particular customer, the sales rep will maximize the average sales per call by calling between 10 and 18 times per quarter—say, 13 times per quarter, or once a week.

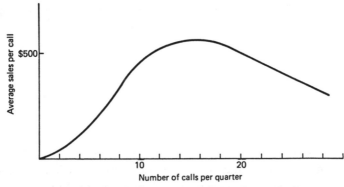

FIGURE 20-2 Projected average sales per call.

The "IFUM" Principle

Theoretically, there is a different expectancy curve as shown in Figure 20-2 for every customer and prospect in the territory—big ones for big customers, small ones for smaller customers. The optimum call frequency might be 5 times per quarter for one, 9 for another, 17 for still another, and so on.

But since it would be virtually impossible for the sales rep to zigzag around the territory to make planned calls with widely varying frequency, it is far more practical to lump customers and prospects into three categories; those to be called on most frequently, less frequently, and least frequently.

If we name these categories A, B, and C, the sales rep will call on A customers and prospects twice as often as B's, and B's twice as often as C's. If he or she can see each A customer once a week, the B's will be seen every other week and each C customer approximately once in four weeks. Or it might be A's every two weeks, B's every four weeks, C's every eight weeks.

Note that we are mingling customer and prospect calls. While the rep is in one part of the territory, scheduled calls are made to both customers and prospects in that area. This saves time and mileage, as compared with the method used by some companies of asking sales reps to set aside one day or a half-day a week for prospect calls.

How many customers and prospects go into each of the A, B, and C pigeonholes? Here we call upon the principle of "ifum"—the *important few and unimportant many.* J. M. Juran, an industrial engineer, reports that in most industries (Figure 20-3) the top 15 percent of the customers produce 65 percent of the total sales volume, the next 20 percent produce another 20 percent and the lowest 65 percent of the customers altogether produce only 15 percent of total volume—or total profit, or total units, or however productivity is measured.

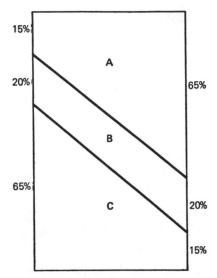

FIGURE 20-3 The Juran diagram illustrating the principle of the "important few and the unimportant many."

The sales rep should first of all make sure that this principle applies in the assigned territory, by ranking the customers and seeing what percentage of total volume is produced by the top 15 percent. It will usually be between 55 and 75 percent or more.

If the rep finds that the top 15 percent produce 50 percent or less of the sales, that means that in this territory the important few are a bit less important and the unimportant many relatively more important. In this case we recommend a two-category allocation method, discussed later.

In the A-B-C method, the sales rep is essentially using a four-cycle planning method; that is, every time four cycles are made throughout the territory, the rep will call on every A customer or prospect four times, each B customer twice, and each C customer once.

To determine how many customers can be placed in each category, the rep first decides how often it is necessary to call on most of the A accounts. The rep may have one or two "super A's" that demand more frequent attention, but what's the standard call frequency for most of the A's?

If the rep sees them once a week, a four-week cycle is in effect: On each *weekly* swing through the territory, the rep sees all the A's, half the B's, and about 25 percent of the C's. The next week, the rep sees all the A's again, the *other* half of the B's, and a new 25 percent of the C's. The following week the rep sees all the A's, the first half of the B's for the second time this cycle, and a new 25 percent of the C's. During the fourth week, the sales rep sees all the A's again, the second half of the B's for the second time, and the remaining 25 percent of the C's.

Thus in every four-week cycle the rep sees all A's four times, all B's twice, and all C's once. (There may be some "sub C's" to be seen less frequently.)

If the rep decides basically to see the A customers every two weeks, an eight-week cycle is in effect—A's are seen every two weeks, B's every four weeks, C's every eight weeks.

Having decided on the basic frequency of A account calls, the rep now estimates how many planned sales calls can be made per four-week or eight-week cycle. The rep simply takes the average number of calls per week and multiplies them by four or eight as the case may be. If some percentage of the time must be spent making emergency deliveries, handling service calls, or collecting delinquent accounts, time is subtracted for those when estimating how many planned sales calls can be made per week.

What percentage of calls goes to A's, B's, and C's? If the rep has, for example, 100 accounts, the percentages work out as shown in Table 20-1.

No matter how many calls the rep estimates he or she can make in each cycle, the percentages in the right-hand column of Table 20-1 hold true. To get the number of A accounts which can be handled, the rep multiplies total calls per cycle by 0.36; this gives the total number of *calls* on all A accounts. Since the rep will be seeing each A account four times, that figure is then divided by four and rounded off to get the number of A's.

For example, if the rep plans to see A accounts every week and can make 20 calls per week, or 80 calls in a four-week cycle, the following computation can be done: 80 x 0.36 = 28.8 calls on A accounts, divided by 4 = 7.2, or 7 A accounts.

A table like Table 20-2 can be used in determining how many accounts to put into each category.

Several questions may have occurred to the reader. One is, "Why allocate 40 percent of calls to the C accounts if they produce only 15 percent of the sales volume?" The answer is that in addition to potential additional business from some small accounts, the small accounts inevitably take more time per sales dollar than the larger accounts, which buy in larger quantities and have more efficient purchasing procedures. The smaller customers do require a certain amount of attention if they are not to be lost to competitors.

TABLE 20-1   Frequency of Calls

Type of account	Number in this category	Calls on each per cycle	Total calls on this category per cycle	Approximate percentage of total calls
A	15	4	60	36
B	20	2	40	24
C	65	1	65	40

TABLE 20-2 Determining Numbers in Each Category (Total
number of scheduled calls on four swings through territory: _____)

Type of account	Multiply total number of calls by	And enter result here	Divide by	Round off and enter here
A	0.36		4	
B	0.24		2	
C	0.40		1	

The mistake many sales reps make is to call on all accounts
with approximately equal frequency, thus investing about 65
percent of their calls on the C accounts.

Another question is, "What about vacations and holidays?"
For purposes of planning sales call allocation, it is easiest to
simply ignore vacations and allocate 100 percent of the time.
After a vacation the reps can simply pick up where they left off (if
no other reps have been covering for them).

When there's a one-day holiday, the reps can simply skip the
calls they would have made that day, contacting the important
customers by phone a day or two before. This is better than
picking up the interrupted cycle the day after the holiday and
thereafter making all calls one day later. The former method has
the advantage of keeping all calls on each major customer on
the same day of the week.

If the reps find that the top 15 percent of their customers give
them only 50 percent or less of their volume, it is more effective
and simpler to use only two frequency categories, A and B.

If they see each A account once a week, they'll see each B
every other week and be on a two-week cycle. If they see A
accounts every two weeks, they'll be on a four-week cycle.

If the reps put 25 percent of their customers in the A

category and 75 percent in the B group, the formula for determining how many can be handled in each group is:

- Estimate total number of sales calls per cycle (two swings around the territory).

- Multiply the total by 0.6. This is the number of calls to be made on A accounts. Divide this number by 2 to get the number of A accounts.

- Multiply the number of A accounts by 3 to get the number of B accounts.

ASSIGNING CUSTOMERS TO CATEGORIES

If sales reps using the A-B-C or 4-2-1 method can make 100 calls a cycle (four swings), they'll find that they can handle 9 A's, 12 B's, and 39 C's. Which accounts and prospects go into each category?

One method is simply to use judgment. Just consider each account and decide whether it's worth one call a week, one call every two weeks, or one call a month. It helps to buy a package of 3 x 5 inch index cards, write the name of a customer or prospect on each, and simply sort them into piles of the predetermined size.

If the rep wishes to back up his or her judgment with a bit of mathematics, a preliminary rating can be made on the basis of the present *and potential* volume of each account, and then any adjustments dictated by individual customers' wants and needs can be made.

To estimate each account's potential, the sales rep fills out a card like this on each account:

Account name: _____

1. Present sales volume, on
   an annualized basis: $_____

2. Estimated additional business available: $_____

3. My chances of getting it,
   expressed as a fraction
   (e.g., a one-third chance
   = 0.33):   _____

4. Expected value of this potential additional business
   (2) x (3): $_____

5. Total present and potential
   future value of this account (1) + (4): $_____

This method has the advantage of integrating customers and prospects into the call frequency pattern.

> For example, a customer may be purchasing $2,500 a year but have no potential for additional sales. A nonbuying prospect has the potential of buying $10,000 a year, but the

sales rep figures his or her chance of getting that account is only 1 in 4, or 0.25. The expected value of the prospect is thus $10,000 x 0.25 = $2,500, which says the prospect should be called upon about as frequently as the customer.

Customers and prospects are preliminarily sorted into the A, B, and C categories on the basis of the figure representing total present and potential future value. Thereafter, some may be upgraded or downgraded on the basis of such considerations as:

1. How often does the customer wish to be called upon?

2. What's the minimum number of calls I need to make to hold the customer's business at present level?

3. What are the customer's buying habits?

4. How much time will it take me to develop the additional volume?

When these adjustments have been made, each account gets an A, B, or C rating that reflects *optimum call frequency*, not just present volume.

If different products within the line vary considerably in profitability, this of course would be taken into consideration in assigning call frequencies. One dollar's worth of a less-profitable product might be counted as only 50 or 75 cents in working out the potential value of the account.

ROUTING

A big advantage of this method is that the sales rep, instead of deciding each Friday night where to call next week or deciding each evening on whom to call next day, can plan his or her routing and calls once and for all, subject to a revision of customer classifications perhaps once a quarter.

The easiest method is to get a map and write on it an A at the location of each A customer, a B at each B customer, and a C for each C customer. One may prefer to use different colored dots to represent the three categories.

Since the reps will be seeing all A customers and prospects on each swing through the territory, they simply set up routes that cover all the A's. As mentioned earlier, on each swing the reps see all A's, half the B's (alternating), and about one-quarter of the C's.

To keep a very simple record of the customers he or she has seen or missed on previous swings through the territory, the rep will find it well worthwhile to list, for each day's routing, all the A's, B's, and C's in that vicinity. Figure 20-4 is an example of such a form, as used by a major feed company. There is a column for each week. At the end of each day, it takes the sales rep about 10 seconds to fill in the appropriate circle in that week's column opposite each account seen that day. If any customer who should have been called on has been missed for some reason, the gap is instantly apparent on the chart.

SOME VARIATIONS

The sales call allocation method just described applies primarily to sales reps who spend most of their time calling on established customers, with some percentage of calls earmarked for prospects.

Other types of selling vary considerably, but the same basic principles can be applied to maximize the return per selling hour. In some cases it is profitable to assign A, B, and C priorities to functions, rather than to accounts.

For example, a sales rep selling annual renewable contracts, such as workmen's compensation insurance, must spend a certain percentage of working time servicing present customers and handling contract renewals, but also cannot neglect the

CUSTOMERS AND PROSPECTS IN THIS PART OF TERRITORY

A's first
B's second
C's third

Sales Call Checkoff

NAMES	JUNE	JULY	AUGUST	SEPTEMBER	OCTOBER	NOVEMBER
_____	o o o o o	o o o o o	o o o o o	o o o o o	o o o o o	o o o o o
_____	o o o o o	o o o o o	o o o o o	o o o o o	o o o o o	o o o o o
_____	o o o o o	o o o o o	o o o o o	o o o o o	o o o o o	o o o o o
_____	o o o o o	o o o o o	o o o o o	o o o o o	o o o o o	o o o o o
_____	o o o o o	o o o o o	o o o o o	o o o o o	o o o o o	o o o o o
_____	o o o o o	o o o o o	o o o o o	o o o o o	o o o o o	o o o o o
_____	o o o o o	o o o o o	o o o o o	o o o o o	o o o o o	o o o o o
_____	o o o o o	o o o o o	o o o o o	o o o o o	o o o o o	o o o o o
_____	o o o o o	o o o o o	o o o o o	o o o o o	o o o o o	o o o o o
_____	o o o o o	o o o o o	o o o o o	o o o o o	o o o o o	o o o o o
_____	o o o o o	o o o o o	o o o o o	o o o o o	o o o o o	o o o o o
_____	o o o o o	o o o o o	o o o o o	o o o o o	o o o o o	o o o o o
_____	o o o o o	o o o o o	o o o o o	o o o o o	o o o o o	o o o o o
_____	o o o o o	o o o o o	o o o o o	o o o o o	o o o o o	o o o o o
_____	o o o o o	o o o o o	o o o o o	o o o o o	o o o o o	o o o o o
_____	o o o o o	o o o o o	o o o o o	o o o o o	o o o o o	o o o o o
_____	o o o o o	o o o o o	o o o o o	o o o o o	o o o o o	o o o o o
_____	o o o o o	o o o o o	o o o o o	o o o o o	o o o o o	o o o o o
_____	o o o o o	o o o o o	o o o o o	o o o o o	o o o o o	o o o o o
_____	o o o o o	o o o o o	o o o o o	o o o o o	o o o o o	o o o o o
_____	o o o o o	o o o o o	o o o o o	o o o o o	o o o o o	o o o o o
_____	o o o o o	o o o o o	o o o o o	o o o o o	o o o o o	o o o o o
_____	o o o o o	o o o o o	o o o o o	o o o o o	o o o o o	o o o o o
_____	o o o o o	o o o o o	o o o o o	o o o o o	o o o o o	o o o o o
_____	o o o o o	o o o o o	o o o o o	o o o o o	o o o o o	o o o o o
_____	o o o o o	o o o o o	o o o o o	o o o o o	o o o o o	o o o o o

FIGURE 20-4 Route listing and sales call check-off form.

A's first B's second C's third	**CUSTOMERS AND PROSPECTS IN THIS PART OF TERRITORY** Sales Call Checkoff					
NAMES	**DECEMBER**	**JANUARY**	**FEBRUARY**	**MARCH**	**APRIL**	**MAY**
————	o o o o o	o o o o o	o o o o o	o o o o o	o o o o o	o o o o o
————	o o o o o	o o o o o	o o o o o	o o o o o	o o o o o	o o o o o
————	o o o o o	o o o o o	o o o o o	o o o o o	o o o o o	o o o o o
————	o o o o o	o o o o o	o o o o o	o o o o o	o o o o o	o o o o o
————	o o o o o	o o o o o	o o o o o	o o o o o	o o o o o	o o o o o
————	o o o o o	o o o o o	o o o o o	o o o o o	o o o o o	o o o o o
————	o o o o o	o o o o o	o o o o o	o o o o o	o o o o o	o o o o o
————	o o o o o	o o o o o	o o o o o	o o o o o	o o o o o	o o o o o
————	o o o o o	o o o o o	o o o o o	o o o o o	o o o o o	o o o o o
————	o o o o o	o o o o o	o o o o o	o o o o o	o o o o o	o o o o o
————	o o o o o	o o o o o	o o o o o	o o o o o	o o o o o	o o o o o
————	o o o o o	o o o o o	o o o o o	o o o o o	o o o o o	o o o o o
————	o o o o o	o o o o o	o o o o o	o o o o o	o o o o o	o o o o o
————	o o o o o	o o o o o	o o o o o	o o o o o	o o o o o	o o o o o
————	o o o o o	o o o o o	o o o o o	o o o o o	o o o o o	o o o o o
————	o o o o o	o o o o o	o o o o o	o o o o o	o o o o o	o o o o o
————	o o o o o	o o o o o	o o o o o	o o o o o	o o o o o	o o o o o
————	o o o o o	o o o o o	o o o o o	o o o o o	o o o o o	o o o o o
————	o o o o o	o o o o o	o o o o o	o o o o o	o o o o o	o o o o o
————	o o o o o	o o o o o	o o o o o	o o o o o	o o o o o	o o o o o
————	o o o o o	o o o o o	o o o o o	o o o o o	o o o o o	o o o o o
————	o o o o o	o o o o o	o o o o o	o o o o o	o o o o o	o o o o o
————	o o o o o	o o o o o	o o o o o	o o o o o	o o o o o	o o o o o
————	o o o o o	o o o o o	o o o o o	o o o o o	o o o o o	o o o o o
————	o o o o o	o o o o o	o o o o o	o o o o o	o o o o o	o o o o o

FIGURE 20-4 Continued.

cycle of prospecting, and making initial calls, proposals, follow-up calls, and closes on new prospects. It is sometimes easy to spend too much time comfortably servicing friendly customers, and too little time in the cold, unfriendly world of prospecting.

This sales rep might well assign an A priority to prospecting and making initial calls, scheduling that work ahead of other activities. The various other functions would be given B or C ratings and specific percentages of working time allocated to them.

Sales reps selling very high-ticket, once-only purchases, like turnkey construction contracts or executive airplanes, can similarly assign priorities to the many tasks that come between initial contact and satisfied customer. Buying influences within the prospect company can be categorized as A, B, or C with regard to their importance and the amount of time that needs to be spent with them.

Sometimes the sales rep faces an all-or-nothing situation. When the customer needs a new piece of machinery or a plant modernization job, one sales rep gets it all. In this case the sales rep can estimate the probabilities of getting an order at varying call frequencies. The rep might estimate, for example, that if he or she calls on the prospect only once a quarter, the chances of getting any business would be 1 percent. If the rep calls once a month, the chances of getting an order might be 30 percent; calling once a week might increase the chances to 60 percent.

The rep can then plot curves similar to those in Figures 20-1 and 20-2, using the probability figures instead of sales volume. If the rep does this for three or four sizes or types of customers, the optimum way of dividing the sales calls among each can be estimated.

21

INCENTIVES FOR FIRST-LINE SALES MANAGERS

The title varies in different industries. The person may be called district manager, division manager, or regional manager. Whatever the title, thc first-line sales manager has a key role in supervising and motivating the sales reps. Most companies, therefore, feel that their field sales managers should also participate in the incentive program, although the plan for them may differ from that of the sales reps.

Designing this plan is difficult if the manager is a part-time manager and part-time sales rep, with account responsibility. If the manager gets a commission or bonus on sales, he or she is likely to neglect field work with sales reps unless the manager also receives some kind of override on their results.

More frequently, the first-line manager can spend 100 percent of the time managing. If the usual number of sales reps—generally from eight to eleven—reports to the manager, and if the manager spends two to four days a week out in the field with them, he or she cannot also be the senior sales rep in the district. (Some companies assign just a few typical accounts to the managers to keep them current on customer reactions and problems.)

The manager's incentive can be based either on total district performance, or on the total incentives earned by his salespersons. If total district performance is the basis, profitability, as contrasted with sales volume, is likely to be more important in the manager's goals than in the sales reps'. As a rule, the manager's incentive plan is designed to provide a total potential income 15 to 50 percent greater than the total income of the median sales rep.

A manufacturer of custom-designed process equipment offers its district managers a bonus of up to 40 percent of their salaries, based on these factors:

Factors	% of maximum bonus
District quota performance	50
District selling expense bonus	10
Special assignment bonus	10
Discretionary bonus (including profitability)	30
	100

This plan has been in effect for more than 20 years. During this period the maximum bonus was increased from an initial 20 percent of salary to the present 40 percent.

In another company, the district manager's bonus is based on the percentage of quotas attained in both sales volume and district profit. The plan is unusual in that the bonus is scaled first up, then down—the former to maximize motivation up to a point, the latter to put somewhat of a ceiling on excessive earnings.

The bonus is calculated as follows:

% of quota	Sales % of salary per quota point	Net profits % of salary per quota point
0– 80	0	0
80– 90	0.1	0.3
90–110	0.25	0.75
110–120	0.1	0.3
Over 120	0.05	0.1

This industry is highly volatile, and branch managers are accustomed to this. Bonus limitations cause no resentment. About half the managers reach their limits regularly.
Limits: 40 percent of salary and 10 percent of profit.

If the first-line manager's incentive is based on incentive earnings of the sales reps instead of total district performance, there is usually some provision that 80 or 100 percent of those reps must achieve quota in order for the manager to qualify for the incentive. Otherwise, the manager might tend to neglect territories far behind quota, where additional effort would not increase total incentive payments in the district. It is possible to work out a managers' compensation plan in which a portion is based on overall profitability of the district and a portion paid on achievements of individual sales reps.

Here is an example where the principles of this are shown:

An Incentive Payable Semiannually on Sales Volume

% range half-year quota	Incentive % of half-yearly salary for each point in bracket
80–95	0.4
95–105	1.0
Over 105	0.4

An Incentive Payable Annually Based on District Profits

% range budgeted profits	Incentive % of annual salary for each point in bracket
0–80	0
80–90	0.15
90–110	0.375
110–120	0.15
120	0.05

This plan-in-principle provided two payments (semiannual and annual) in order to accord with the company's accounting system, since profitability could more accurately be measured against a year's results. No limit was proposed because where a plan like this was installed, district profits were seldom volatile. The principles could be employed by almost any company, varying the payout standards and rates according to its situation.

The authors favor the principle of paying managers more like executives, at least in certain situations. Extra discretionary awards for superior achievements in personnel management, development, improved share of market, and similar accomplishments have achieved gratifying results for some of the companies that have used them in a well-planned, carefully monitored manner.

The procedure for developing a manager's sales incentive plan is exactly the same as that for the sales reps—select the income parameters, decide on the split between guaranteed and contingent components, devise a formula, test it, then repeat the procedure until a satisfactory result is obtained.

22

SALES COMPENSATION PLANS FOR WHOLESALERS AND DISTRIBUTORS

A "stocking" wholesaler or distributor—that is, one who buys merchandise, warehouses it, sells it to retailers or users, delivers it, and extends credit to customers—usually gets a markup of 10 to 30 percent or more on the products. The margin varies considerably from industry to industry, and with the cost and value of the services provided by the wholesaler. The individual wholesaler usually gets different markups on different lines, the amount often influenced by the direct costs of handling and selling the items. A commission based solely on the selling price would be too large on some lines and too small on others, because of these varying margins. Most wholesalers, therefore, pay the salesperson some percentage of the wholesaler's markup.

The plan is easy to administer and does motivate sales reps to concentrate on the high margin lines and to maintain the listed prices—since price cuts, if sanctioned, come partly out of the sales rep's pocket. This type of plan also is nearly standard in many industries, and is hence readily accepted by the sales force.

A possible disadvantage of such a plan lies in the fact that, as noted in Chapter 7, the higher margin lines may not be the ones making the greatest profit contribution. If the lines involve high direct costs—inventory space, selling time, delivery charges, customer service, billing costs—they may be less profitable than lines with a lower margin and lower direct costs.

One approach might be to group the product lines into three or four categories based on profitability, and pay an incentive weighted by profitability, as described in Chapter 15. Little attention has been paid to this possibility in most areas of wholesaling.

USAGE

In answer to our survey of methods of compensating their sales representatives, one hundred twenty-seven distributors and wholesalers responded as follows. (Percentages should be interpreted with caution because of the small number of cases.)

- 53.9% paid salary plus incentive.

- 23.8% paid commission with a drawing account.

- 15.8% paid commission with no drawing account.

- 6.5% paid straight salary.

Thus, the tendency is for distributors and wholesalers to have roughly similar preferences as to basic type of sales compensation as manufacturers. These preferences must be considered in light of the many and diverse types of distributors sampled, ranging from wholesalers of industrial supplies to alcoholic beverages, and from distributors of jewelry to pharmaceuticals, toys, and office equipment.

Although the subsamples are too small for statistically reliable judgments to be made, dissatisfaction seems relatively high with straight salary plans (44.4 percent) and salary-plus-incentive plans (22.7 percent).

For most wholesalers and distributors, retaining professional compensation assistance may seem unwarranted, yet the typical complaints regarding type of plan used are similar to those raised by manufacturers using such plans:

Users of salary plus incentive typically complain about:

- The difficulty of equating sales volume and profitability

- The difficulty of achieving equitable territorial and customer assignments

- The administrative burdens required by most plans

Users of commission plans typically complain that:

- It is frequently difficult for new sales representatives to get started unless given a draw.

- Control over the sales representatives' efforts is sometimes weak.

- Inequitable and unequal territorial and customer assignments often exist.

Most of the users of straight salary, while endorsing the control this pay method gives them, mention its lack of motivation as a disadvantage.

It is not possible to offer constructive sales incentive compensation advice to distributors and wholesalers as a group. As individual entities, however, most of their problems seem manageable. A few suggestions follow.

> Computer calculation of gross margins by product lines might well serve either as a sales performance standard (quota), or as a factor to weight dollar sales quotas. Products with similar gross margins might be grouped. Admittedly, this could be expensive, especially for the small wholesaler. It would surely add to the administrative headaches, and probably lessen the sales reps' understanding of the plan. Maybe these disadvantages are worth what they cost.

Salary administration, as conducted by many wholesalers, can probably be improved. Suggestions along these lines were offered in Chapter 18. Many of these could be used by wholesalers.

Users of pay plans based heavily upon commission might benefit by emulating the precepts followed by some of the life insurance companies and certain computer manufacturers.

> Oversimplified, these plans pay the sales rep a straight salary for a period sufficient to get started, then offer him or her a modest commission, at the same time reducing the salary slightly. Ultimately, the objective is to get the sales rep on a straight commission basis (in the life insurance field), or nearly so.

> Good producers under such plans are never asked to take a step backward in income, only to accept more risk in return for a chance for bigger earnings through higher commission rates.

A variation of this approach is to offer higher commission rates if the rep will accept a higher quota.

Wholesalers in service industries also report problems in providing their sales reps with incentive compensation, probably because of the diversity of those businesses polled in the survey (ranging from selling financial and engineering services to producing specialized mill products). Dissatisfaction was highest among those paying salary plus incentive, and those paying their reps straight salaries. These distributors—if they should offer an incentive increment at all (and certainly not all of them should do so)—might consider the method certain life insurance companies and computer manufacturers use in paying their reps, as described in this chapter.

23

SALES COMPENSATION PLANS FOR RETAILERS

Each type of retailing tends to develop its own customs with regard to sales compensation. Auto dealers and real estate firms tend to pay on a straight commission basis; grocers and druggists usually pay straight salaries. For years, most department stores paid straight salaries in all departments except furniture, carpets, and major appliances, which were on a commission basis. In all departments there were sometimes "spiffs" or "PMs" (for "push money" or "promotional money")—nominal sums paid by the manufacturer whenever the sales clerk sold its product.

Considering all types of retailers, the most commonly used sales compensation is probably salary plus commission. Where traffic is heavy and sales volume high, salaries tend to be the smaller portion of total compensation (unions often participate in establishing salary levels). Commissions tend to vary with the gross margin or profit of the items sold. Most retail personnel have a good idea of the relative profitability of the lines they handle.

In some fashion-oriented retail establishments, salaries are a larger portion of total earnings, but even so are unlikely to be more than a basic living wage; commissions are still an important factor in the total earnings package. Commissions are sometimes pooled, sometimes paid on the basis of individual sales, sometimes determined by both individual performance and total department performance.

One of the difficult problems the retail manager has in using any type of incentive plan is in making sure that each salesperson has an equal opportunity at the big sales and the busy selling hours.

Gasoline service stations (in normal times) represented a field of retailing where, historically, incentive programs sometimes increased profit remarkably. For most stations, sales of oil and gas "paid the rent," and the real profits were made by building up volume in TBA—tires, batteries, and accessories.

The service station attendants often have a major influence on TBA sales. If alert, they can spot damaged tires, worn wiper blades, weak batteries, bad fan belts, and many other defects. Stations which pay attendants some kind of commission on TBA sales usually show increases in such sales—and it is notable that incentives paid on the basis of individual performance are almost always more effective than those paid on a pooled basis.

An incentive that was long popular with service stations was something like this:

- No commission on gasoline or oil

- 1 percent commission on a lubrication job

- 3 percent commission on sales of filters, belts, and tires
- 5 percent commission on sales of batteries, antifreeze, wiper blades, and similar products

In the more recent "gas-and-go" environment, the practice of paying incentives may have languished, but it may be resumed if supplies permit.

A recent (1979) confidential survey of retailers in a major eastern city (some 60 stores) shows the following:

Type of establishment	Sales personnel compensation
High fashion stores	$2.90 to $3.50 per hour + 1 to 5% commission. Average is $3.20 + 3%.*
Middle range retailers (various lines)	$2.90 to $5.50 per hour + commission, varying with department. Typical case is $2.90 + 5% commission on sales over $700 weekly.

In the middle-range sample (20 stores) some sales personnel get a minimum salary plus a drawing account. (Commissions tend to be higher with no draw, and on some lines, e.g., Misses' coats, 6 percent.)

Type of establishment	Sales personnel compensation
Appliances (stores and departments)	Commonly on minimum hourly rate + 2 to 7% commission. Commission varies with the product and the store.
Discount department stores	$3 to $5 per hour + commission. Rates vary from one store to another, and according to department to which salesperson is assigned. Sales clerks "stretched out" to cover more than one department are paid slightly higher rates.*
	$3.00 + 5% commission is a typical median pay package.

*All these salary rates will probably be increased by minimum wage legislation, as it takes effect.

No variation was reported according to store location—neighborhood stores versus downtown stores versus malls. While equalizing of prime selling time was not reported in the survey, it is, of course, commonly practiced.

Incentives are less likely to be paid when the retail personnel are routine order-takers, such as those accepting clothing at a dry-cleaner, and are more likely to be paid when the salesperson can exert a big influence on the size and type of product or service the customer selects.

An interesting example of the latter is the retail travel agency. The inside salespersons often have an opportunity to "trade up" a prospect from a simple airline ticket to a more profitable cruise or packaged tour. The agency receives commissions of 7 to 15 percent on the various travel services it sells. Since it is relatively easy to calculate the commissions earned by each employee, an incentive plan can be based on individual productivity.

About one-fourth of all retail travel agencies have some type of incentive payment plan. An ingenious one is to offer the employee some percentage, say 30 percent of the agency's commission, after the total commissions brought in by the employee amount to three times his or her salary. (Depending upon salary level, the figure could vary from 2½ to 3½ times salary.) Since salaries represent about 50 percent of the total costs of an agency, an employee earning a salary of $6,000, for example, would have to bring in $18,000 in commissions before earning an incentive. That $18,000 covers the individual's salary, an equal amount contributed to overhead, and an equal amount again contributed to agency profit.

In any plan in which retail salespersons are paid on the basis of individual sales, the question arises as to who gets credit for the sale in certain situations.

In the case of a travel agency, for example, suppose a couple have come in three or four times to discuss possible cruises, and one of the counselors has spent a great deal of time helping them make a selection. On the day the couple come in to book the cruise and make a deposit, their counselor is out to lunch and another employee handles the booking. Who should be credited for the sale?

There are three ways of handling such questions, and they apply to any type of retail establishment:

1. Trust the employees to use common sense in deciding among themselves who gets credit for a sale. If the staff is friendly and not too greedy, this works well.

2. Devise some very simple rule of thumb, such as: The sale goes to the employee who gets the deposit, or to the employee who first speaks to the customer. This will result in obvious unfairness in some instances, but in the long run the good and bad breaks tend to even out.

3. Devise elaborate and complete rules for determining what percentage of each sale goes to each person when two or more have participated in it.

Along the latter lines, Earl Harmon of Harmon Travel in Boise, Idaho, whose employees are all on a salary plus commission basis, has devised complete rules governing such splits. On a cruise sale, for example, 10 percent of the credit goes to the employee who contacts the client, 15 percent to the one who gets the client to select the cruise, 10 percent to the one handling the booking, and so on.

The retailer, however small, can follow the same principles which this book recommends for large corporations, especially:

1. Be careful to define the objective of the incentive plan. Is it intended to increase sales volume in general, to encourage the sale of add-ons, to ensure the upgrading of customers to more expensive merchandise, to bring in new customers, or what?

2. Decide whether the objectives of the plan (including ease of administration) will be more effectively met by a pooled plan, or by one in which each person is rewarded for individual achievement.

3. Pretest the plan on paper. How will it affect profits if there is a boom? A bust? If one salesperson triples his or her sales volume? If there is a marked increase or decrease in the demand for one type of product?

Retail customers can at times be difficult and demanding; a financial reward for successful salesmanship makes it easier for salespeople to maintain both the customer relations and the sales results the store owner desires.

INDEX

ABOUT THE AUTHORS

John W. Barry, a marketing and sales compensation consultant and a cum laude graduate in economics from Harvard, has designed some 150 sales compensation programs for clients in four countries. He has conducted many seminars on sales incentive compensation and has written extensively on marketing and compensation subjects for such publications as *Sales & Marketing Management, Printers' Ink, Business Management, Industrial Marketing, Technica et Organizatione, Chemical Week,* and others.

Porter Henry has produced sales training materials and conducted sales meetings for several hundred top U.S. firms. A Phi Beta Kappa graduate of Washington University in St. Louis, he founded Porter Henry & Co., Inc., a leading sales and marketing consulting firm, in 1945. He too has written a great deal on sales, compensation, marketing, and other business subjects.